Free for All

Free for All

Oddballs, Geeks, and Gangstas in the Public Library

Don Borchert

Distributed by Holtzbrinck Publishers

Designed by Jason Snyder

Library of Congress Cataloging-in-Publication Data

Borchert, Don.
  Free for all : oddballs, geeks, and gangstas in the public library / Don Borchert.
      p. cm.
  Includes bibliographical references.
  ISBN-13: 978-1-905264-12-4
  ISBN-10: 1-905264-12-7
  1. Borchert, Don. 2. Public librarians–California–Biography. 3. Public libraries–California–Anecdotes. 4. Library users–California–Anecdotes.
  I. Title.
  Z720.B725A3 2007
  020.92–dc22
  [B]
                              2007036107

  ISBN-13: 978-1-9052-6412-4
  ISBN-10: 1-9052-6412-7

10 9 8 7 6 5 4 3 2 1

Author's Note

THIS IS A WORK OF NONFICTION based on my experiences working in the library for the past god-knows-how-many years. With the exception of Terri, Curtis, and Carla, whose real names appear in the book, I have changed names and some personal characteristics and have altered certain incidents to protect the privacy of those involved and so that my friends and colleagues will continue to offer me jelly doughnuts and warm English muffins on the mornings they bring them in.

To friends and family.

To Sally and Andrea and Beth and Rosie, and to my dad.

To Bob and Donna Perkins.

To Ian Morgan, John Kalmbaugh, and Tom Ryan—
oh my, what a bunch. Big, tough ones.

To Theresa and Curtis Babiar and Rhea Edelman,
library stalwarts.

To Greg Bobulinski, jazz trumpet player extraordinaire,
who reminds us that life is not merely endless commerce.

To Lynne Wolverton.

"The secondhandedness of the learned world is the secret of its mediocrity."

—ALFRED NORTH WHITEHEAD

Contents

Acknowledgments

To Randi Murray, literary agent, who is optimistic and persistent where I am not.

To the city of Torrance, for supplying more than a decade of employment, office supplies, and a never-ending source of good material, and to the good people who work for the city.

To the city of Lomita, for allowing me to play the accordion in its library for seven years.

To Carla Sedlacek, one of the great children's librarians.

To Marc Haeringer, editor, who tried to make me look thoughtful and coherent.

To Ken Siman, publisher.

Thank you.

Introduction

LIBRARIES ARE A FOOTNOTE to our civilization, an outpost to those unfamiliar with the concept, and a cheap, habit-forming narcotic to the regular patron. Walk into a public library and it is usually as calm and inviting as a warm bath. It is clean, well kept, and quiet enough to do the Sunday crossword puzzle (the one you brought with you from home, not the one torn surreptitiously out of the library's copy of the paper while no one was looking) with minimal interruption. The staff is invariably professional, courteous, and unobtrusive. They are almost always educated — not just disillusioned college grads who could find nothing in their own field but majors in Library Science, a degree as arcane as alchemy or predicting the future by reading the entrails of a recently slaughtered lamb.

There are comfortable chairs scattered throughout the facility, and nice wooden worktables to spread out your things. There is no admission charge, and it has always been a clean, well-lit place to come into out of the rain during a heavy thunderstorm. The floors are vacuumed regularly, the restrooms have been thoroughly disinfected and cleaned in the last twelve hours, and there is usually soap in the hand-soap dispenser and paper towels in the paper-towel dispenser. I will put myself out on a limb and say that more than 99 percent of public libraries in this country are heated in the winter and cooled in the summer. This is not done for the sake of the books. The library is trying to welcome you.

Put five books together on a shelf and you have a library. Add another 20,000 volumes and you still have a library—a bigger one, though not necessarily a better one. If all the Library of Alexandria in Egypt had on its shelves when it burned to the ground were Harlequin romances and a few dog-eared Max Brand novels, it would have been a far lesser tragedy. But it was rumored they had good stuff. A public library embodies the same idea, but people can walk in off the street, pull the books off the shelf without an employee looking nervously over their shoulders, and take them home. All you have to do is promise to bring them back.

A library is an idea more than anything else, and it is an idea that is impossible to swallow in one or two big bites. The library is patrician, elitist, and democratic, stocking biographies of NASCAR drivers, pornography, antidemocratic literature, comic books, and the works of the great thinkers from the past two thousand years. Once a book hits the shelf, the library is loath to get rid of it no matter what outrage it causes. The only way a library will discard a book is if it is ignored. The scandalous ones do not get ignored until they are passé.

The library offers books on every subject imaginable, in a variety of languages, and offers state-of-the-art computers with free word processing and Internet services. A mecca for scholars and students of all ages, the library is the dullest place in the world—91 percent of the time. It also attracts the homeless, the mentally ill, occasional pedophiles, Internet junkies, unattended children down to the age of two, con artists, thieves, beggars, cultish homeschoolers, and people who are in general angry with every level of state and federal government. Most of these people decide to fill out an application and get a library card.

This makes librarians inordinately happy. We love seeing new patrons wandering around, browsing, looking at what's on the shelves.

Why?

Because there is a belief that once you begin to open books, you will become a better person. It is Pandora's box, but in a good

XV

way. You are inching toward the promised land, page by page. And it doesn't matter if you subscribe to this theory or not. The subscription has already been bought and paid for.

We are all misfits, poseurs, and clowns. We are heartbroken and lonely, failures in life, criminals and frauds. Most of our successes are pleasant illusions. Through the books on the shelves, the library becomes a support group and lets us know that we are not alone. Once we realize we are not alone, we can relax, set our burdens down, and move on.

Support your local library.

Get a library card.

Pay your goddamn fines. Man up for Christ's sake. Be a little responsible.

And if there's any shushing to be done, let it be done by a professional.

Me.

Chapter One
A Civil Servant Is Born

I WAS SINGLE ONCE, AND YOUNG. I took jobs that amused me or offered themselves to me, and I walked around with a paycheck in my pocket, happy as a clam and living like a baron until my pockets were empty and I was broke. I thought this was the way to live, and I got away with it for years. I worked in a record store and listened to music all day long and sold Supertramp and Grateful Dead albums to cute girls in tie-dyed shirts and ragged, low-cut jeans. I became the classical music salesman, because I was the only one in the store besides the manager who knew how many symphonies Beethoven had written, and I could recommend a really good *Swan Lake* (Ansermet conducting the Suisse Romande Orchestra). There were, however, more gaps in my knowledge than there was knowledge. I didn't know a thing about composers like Haydn or Mahler or Scarlatti, and I certainly couldn't recommend specific performances or record labels. Luckily, people who asked for this kind of music usually had definite preferences, and I'd listen to them attentively, nodding at appropriate places, until I had milked them dry.

I was fired from the record store for my nonchalance. We had a big problem with shrinkage—merchandise walking out the door not having been paid for—and the manager figured it had to be me. It wasn't. It was Manny, the in-house big-band specialist, whose pot consumption was making him far more nonchalant than I could ever be. I figured the manager's mistake would dawn on him when the shrinkage continued long after I was history.

I worked as a proofreader for a religious publishing company. I also worked on a sod farm, folding slices of thick, green sod on large pallets. I was a grill chef at a very nice restaurant in Columbus, Ohio. I hauled trucks of fill dirt to level out a low-lying, boggy area at a local cemetery—the bog was hurting sales. I worked for the Ford Motor Company testing water pumps and flywheels, whatever they are. I worked the midnight shift at a convenience store in suburban Cleveland, where every so often the pay phone in the front of the store would start ringing around 3:00 a.m., and someone identifying himself as a policeman would suggest that I lock the front door for fifteen minutes or so, because two individuals—white, male, early twenties—were holding up convenience stores in my area in a primer-coated Camaro and pistol-whipping the clerks. I'd lock the front door and hide in the walk-in cooler for an hour until my teeth started chattering, wondering how I had come to such a point in my life.

For an ungodly stretch of time, I worked for a corporation that owned thousands of apartments and condos across the state, and all I did was change out cracked and vandalized commodes. I explained to the foreman that I had no particular expertise in this field, and he replied sagely: "After fifty or sixty of them, you'll get a handle on it." He was absolutely correct.

I did not mind terrible jobs, earning terrible wages, and I didn't mind sleeping in the back of my car, which I did for a few months. I was young and single, and having the time of my life. I did not see married life as the next logical step, but that's what happened. I became part of a couple, so there was another person to care for and to think about and everything changed. We shared a bathroom, an apartment, pondered the relative merit of different-colored bath towels, bought a welcome mat, shopped for groceries, and wound up adopting a kitten whose previous owners kept him outside at night in the bottom of an empty fifty-five-gallon drum.

How did I feel about children, about having one of my own? It had never occurred to me before. But holding my first newborn baby made me happy in a way I could have never imagined. I loved being a father, having a baby fall asleep on my chest and singing sea shanties to her at bedtime. We had two more girls. It was like coming home to Cirque du Soleil every night. And then there were trips to the emergency room, and to the doctor's office, and to schools and to rancorous PTA meetings, and in what seemed like the blink of an eye the carefree days of my youth were gone forever.

I needed to find a real job, anything to stave off creditors and put food on the table. Real jobs may be backbreaking, pointless, and monotonous, but they are always preferable to, say, fleeing from helicopters and foam-flecked hounds in knee-deep, tea-colored water, shackled at the ankles. Real jobs have starting times, written descriptions, salary ranges, dental coverage, and holidays. A real job is something someone else would gladly do if you threw up your hands and decided that it was too much for you.

A real job is working in the private sector for people who have painstakingly built a business and expect it to make a profit. More often than not, a company will jettison most of its employees just to keep the company alive. Or the ownership of the company will change, and the new owners will want to put in their own people, to ensure loyalty. Or the owner will get cancer and say the hell with this, and spend his last few salty crumbs of time sailing the Pacific with his wife, drinking good wine on a small but well-equipped yacht. These are real jobs.

I applied for a position as an advertising manager for one of the heavyweights in the closed circuit television industry. The job seemed like something I could do, even though I had never done such a thing before. At the interview I was very confident—at least as confident as the applicants who *had* done such a thing before but were bridling at the ridiculously low starting salary. My totally unfounded confidence and willingness to accept substandard wages put me ahead of the other candidates, and I got the job. The whole business was cameras. Cameras in the operating room. Cameras in the patient. Cameras in the parking garage. Cameras at the ATM machine. Lots and lots of cameras in the casinos. Cameras watching the babysitter. Cameras making sure that no one was trying to fuck with the other cameras. One morning, the parent company sent two very special messengers to our company, who went in and had a closed-door meeting with the president and, a little more than an hour later, emerged from the meeting, walked the president of the company to his car with a box of his modest belongings, and told him not to come back. Because I had been personally selected by the outgoing president, it was only a matter of time before two lower-echelon messengers walked me to my car, too. I, however, had cleverly been taking office supplies for the previous six weeks, so I knew my pen and pencil and tape expenses would be minimal for some time to come.

So I became Mr. Mom. One of the things I did to make ends meet was to take a job as a "yard lady" at my daughter's elementary school. I was a bulldog of a yard lady, too. I broke up fights between second graders, sent kids to the school nurse for scraped knees, chided them for cheating at dodge ball, and blew a stainless steel whistle whenever I really wanted to get the children's attention. Armed only with this metal whistle, a clipboard, and an all-weather Sharpie—in case I had to write up the more egregious playground violations in the rain—I wielded tremendous but very limited power. I was the biggest and oldest of fish in the smallest and youngest of ponds.

Your quality of life, however, cannot help but go into a quiet and horrible downward spiral when you're grossing sixty dollars a week as a yard lady. It's just not enough these days. After taxes, you are making enough money to treat yourself to a McDonald's Happy Meal every day. Forget about those lottery tickets, birthday presents, groceries, or asthma prescriptions for your child. That kind of life is behind you. There's enough gas to get you to the school and back home again, though you should probably start thinking seriously about walking to the bank to cash that check. The decline in lifestyle is almost imperceptible, tragically graceful, and it would have been hilariously piquant if it were happening to anyone else but me.

One day I had lunch with an old friend of mine, Susan. We both worked at Northrop Electronics in the good old days of aerospace, when the United States thought we'd better fine-tune our missile systems or the Soviet Union would do to us what we were thinking of doing to them. We worked on a classified project called the MX missile system, and the less said about that the better. The MX missile system acted like my stupid dog when I hold out a treat and say "Here, Buddy!" Sometimes the missile worked, sometimes it just sat there, and sometimes it completely ignored me and chewed itself for fleas. When the generals in charge had seen enough, they canceled the project, funneled the money to other spurious projects, and everyone got walked to their cars.

Susan told me that she was applying for a civil service job in the South Bay Library system, a middle-class suburb right next to Los Angeles. How hard could that be? You're in a room full of books. Someone comes in and you let them have a few. You remind them to bring them back. Someone talks too loud and you tell him to knock it off. She suggested I apply for the job, too. I had never entertained a civil service thought in my life.

She said, "The good thing about civil service is that you can fall over and die once you get the job. No one ever quits civil service, and you have to be a fucking idiot to get fired. Just show up every day, on time, until your probationary period is over—like three months— smile at everyone, keep your mouth shut, and you're golden." Susan made it sound simple. "You fill out an application. Take a typing test, get interviewed, give them three references, tell them what they want to hear, and that's it. You're in."

And it was simple. The aerospace application was more than ten pages long and asked you what you were doing twenty years ago. The civil service application was barely a page and a half and virtually multiple choice. Susan listed me as one of her references and I listed her as one of mine.

We both advanced to the typing test. To prepare for this, I bought a software typing program and did the tests and exercises on a home computer until I was cruising along at around 94 words per minute. The library demanded 40 words per minute, which can be managed using two fingers. I intended to smoke all other applicants on this point. The day of the typing test, a group of about twenty of us filed into a dark, dank, windowless basement room and sat at long, formal rows of cute, archaic workstations. This is the last stop on the road to oblivion for obsolete, city-owned computers. After this point, even the elementary schools will make a sour face and decline the donation.

Two minutes into the test a nicely dressed, middle-aged woman next to me let out an audible sigh, took off her glasses, and rubbed her eyes in defeat, shaking her head. She had cracked under the pressure.

Choke!

One less!

Four weeks later, I was invited to an oral interview. I sat across from three somber librarians who had been imported from other library systems to preserve impartiality, shook the hand of one of them, and smiled at the other two, who kept their hands politely in their laps.

What would I do if I thought a patron was intoxicated?

What would I do if I saw a child pulling books off the shelves and ripping pages out?

What would I do if I saw a coworker stealing from the petty cash?

What would I do?

Everyone is asked the same tiresome volley of questions, and I knew the right answer. I'd go to my supervisors and inform them. I'd do the chain-of-command thing. I'd let them make the big decisions.

The interview took ten minutes. At the end, and only then, they relaxed and smiled back at me. They were happy that I had the right answers. Not everyone can be expected to answer this way. Sometimes an interviewee will say that he would throw a person out, grab a person and smack the book out of his hands, call the police, or tackle the prick in the parking lot, and this kind of answer does not make them smile and relax. Loose cannons do not do well as civil servants, and when they are hired it never ends well.

Two weeks later, I was called back for yet another interview. I was asked mostly the same questions, only this time I was talking to the people I might soon be working with. The panel consisted of three older women, all of whom have since retired. Each took a turn reading questions aloud from a clipboard they passed along from person to person. When I responded, they smiled reassuringly and shook their heads warmly. The whole interview was so unnaturally convivial that I wondered if one of the three was training a small handgun on me from underneath the table. But they just wanted to hear the same answers I had given the first time, and more importantly, they wanted to have a warm feeling for the person in front of them. They wanted me to be nicely dressed but not self-consciously formal. Casual but not insouciant. Most of all, relaxed and warm. I was all these things. I knew enough to leave my wise-ass self at home that day.

By the time I got home from the interview, there was a message on my answering machine to report to City Hall to schedule a physical, sign the necessary documents, promise to swear allegiance to the union, and listen to a two-hour presentation on what it was going to be like to work for the city. I showed up at City Hall with an entire gaggle of the newly employed, and after the two-hour presentation a union official showed us a wooden box filled with books and said we would be required to prove that we could lift a similar box at the upcoming mandated physical. Picking up a box is no longer part of the hiring process as it was deemed discriminatory to people who could not pick up the box.

As we filed out, we were informed that we would be getting paid for the time spent in orientation, at whatever our normal hourly rate would be. We were going to get paid for sitting in a room listening to what it was going to be like to be city employees.

Chapter Two
A First Taste of the Library

WHEN I WAS A LITTLE KID, my mom and dad took us to the public library on West 119th Street and Lorain Road in Cleveland. Every Tuesday night. When I got home from school, my mom warned me to get my homework done early, so that when we got back from the library I could sit in bed and read without having to worry about impending schoolwork and unfinished assignments. Not that I was ever plagued with this kind of anxiety. I knew I was plenty smart and could get a C average in most classes just by using a commonsense approach to whatever was being taught. This didn't work in French class, though, where I limped by on my French accent alone, and not by my skills in vocabulary, comprehension, or my ability to conjugate French verbs. The teacher would compliment me on my lovely, authentic French accent, and if I understood what she said I'd smile and respond, "Merci. Il n'y a pas de quoi." Thank you. It was nothing. If I didn't understand what she was saying, I'd just sit there and smile. Either way, in a few seconds, she'd move on. The common-sense thing didn't work in geometry, either. Common sense told me I'd never need geometry again in my life, but the teacher was one of my favorites. I'd sit up front and listen to her talk about the area of a circle, loci, and bisecting angles and parallelograms, and knew I was a lucky young man to have such an inspired teacher go on and on about what was obviously outdated nonsense.

She was kind enough to propose extra-credit projects that would buoy me up enough to get a passing grade, and a few weeks later I brought her an original oil painting, signed, of intersecting spheres, acute angles, and pastel rhomboids, which she admired so much that she put it up in back of the classroom and raised my grade, not to a D but to a C. What a woman.

On Tuesday nights, my mom didn't have to worry about me. Everything was fine, the homework was up to date, and I was always ready for the library.

My dad wasn't much of a reader. He'd sit in the periodical section and page through a copy of *Look* magazine, light up a cigarette, and take long, deep drags, happily and contentedly bored. He didn't go to the library growing up and never really bonded with the institution. His folks owned a *Grapes of Wrath*–style chicken farm on a rural truck route out past the Cleveland suburbs, and his father built a small, cinderblock roadhouse at the front of the property with dreams of selling pitchers of beer, pickled eggs, and fried chicken to hungry travelers. He had many grandiose entrepreneurial schemes that involved my father's unstinting and uncompensated labor, and if he was caught reading a book it meant he was available for chores.

My mom was justifiably terrified of *her* father, a first-generation immigrant from Germany who had grown up during the Great Depression and had lived with bread lines, hunger, and the prospect of losing everything for years. It hardened him and made him brutal, even when the bad times were gone for good, and she took several buses every day to sit in the library and read. It was escape on several levels. She thought of the library as a civilized, elegant place—a place of peace and quiet. My grandfather was wholly unfamiliar with the concept of public libraries, and it never occurred to him to look for her there.

Even before I began to use the library, I had a nice collection of comic books. I preferred Batman to Superman for reasons that, even as a little kid, I thought were painfully obvious. In the overall flow-chart of superheroes, Batman was frail. He was beaten, thrown out of airplanes, kicked down stairs, attacked by guard dogs, and knocked unconscious in almost every issue. Superman was god. As a kid, I could connect with frail. God was unknowable; his problems were not mine. Kryptonite? Give me a break.

I also read Green Lantern, Flash, Blackhawk, and the Justice League of America. Green Arrow had his moments. I never understood the people who followed Superboy, Supergirl, or Wonder Woman. I bought an issue of Little Lulu once, where her house is completely buried under a horrible snowfall and she digs her way out with a cereal spoon. I should have kept that one. Never bought Archie or Jughead, but I was impressed with their cartoon girlfriends' outstanding figures. No Bettys or Veronicas I knew were ever built like that. Soon enough, soon enough, the thirty-two-page comic books were not enough. I craved more. So while my mom wandered through the adult-fiction and non-fiction aisles I stood in the science-fiction section. Books are, after all, much like comic books, but larger, thicker, heavier, and more convoluted. They made better pictures in my head.

I was stunned when I finally read *Dandelion Wine* by Ray Brad-bury. I think it was the first time I read a book and was impressed enough to remember the author's name. I read everything by him. I'd even go out and buy one of the monthly science-fiction magazines, ex-travagant for me, if one of his stories was on the inside. Soon, I drifted into Isaac Asimov, Philip Jose Farmer, and Philip Dick. My mother neither encouraged the reading of science fiction nor did she dispar-age it. She told me later that there was a scheme of things. Young peo-ple were first drawn to fiction, but as they grew older they were pulled more and more into nonfiction and biography, because nonfiction is so much more tragic, engrossing, and hilarious than anything else that could be invented. In this grand scheme, comic books and science fic-tion were just fine. They filled the need for a certain amount of time, and you moved on when that need was no longer filled.

The library ritual for my family continued every Tuesday night for years, and even when I went away to college at Ohio State I knew I could go to the public telephone on the first floor of my dorm, call home on Tuesday night, and no one would answer. My mom's M.O. never changed. Have a highball ready for my dad when he walked in the door around five. Dinner almost immediately thereafter. Then she washed the dishes, and if my dad knew what was good for him, he'd grab a dish towel, dry the dishes, and put them away. She'd comb her hair, reapply her makeup, and put on a coat. Then it was out the door, straight to the library. Check out the new releases, wander through the fiction aisles and take a chance on a female writer she had never tried before, stop at the drugstore on the way home for a carton of smokes and a bar of chocolate, then go back home and stack the books next to the bed. She'd have a smoke, watch the news, eat some chocolate, have a few more smokes, then go to bed. My dad did not read in bed. He hit the pillow and fell asleep snoring. It was one of his great gifts. Mom stayed up for another hour or two reading before she turned out her light.

College was a time of extravagant, undisciplined, and unbounded reading for me. A comparative literature professor would pass out sheets of suggested reading and it was all good stuff. There were textbooks—usually terrible and hardly necessary—but they'd mention some classic I had never heard of, and I would highlight it with a yellow marker as another hot lead. I had a two-fisted, double-martini-drinking Japanese literature professor who radiated gin and a passion for his subject, and his kernel of sorrow lay in the fact that he woke up every morning in mid-Ohio in rented housing across the street from a metal fabrication company, not the rain-slick, red-tiled roofs of rural Kyoto in the Kamakura period. I also had friends who were passionate about books, and they would wake me up in the middle of the night just to tell me about something they had just finished reading.

After college the books no longer found you. You have to go look for them. It is a good thing I work at a library. Mine is a branch library, a smaller satellite to the main library. The branch is an unobtrusive, modest-sized brick building built in the 1960s, and it is identifiable only as a library by the large, permanent concrete sign close to the street that proclaims it as such. There are several similar branches throughout the city. Each one comes with a senior librarian, a children's librarian, a few assistant librarians—like me—and many, many pages who are given the unending task of putting the books back on the shelves so that we can find them again. In my library, we have regular patrons who come in on the same day every week. Some come in every few weeks. A few come in at the same time every day. The regulars invariably read fiction. When someone comes in and wants the automotive manual for the 1987 Toyota Corolla, there is a good chance that it is their first visit to the library in some time. But when someone comes in and asks for the latest Fern Michaels, Tom Clancy, or Cormac McCarthy, you know you have a regular on your hands.

Recently, I witnessed the fiction to nonfiction crossover that my mother had theorized about. A woman, fortyish, came in and said she was sick to death of the detective novels she had once loved and wanted to start reading true crime. One of her friends had recommended starting with a woman writer by the name of Ann Rule. She brought the book back two weeks later and asked for several more by the same woman. I showed her where we keep the true crime books. There is a whole wall of it.

She told me she would make herself some microwavable popcorn, climb into bed, read Ann Rule for forty-five minutes, then hop back out of bed and check to make sure all the doors and windows were locked—such was her fear that some serial killer would crawl out of a nearby swamp and pay her a visit. Years of Dick Francis, Ross Macdonald, and gory detective novels had never instilled the same behavior.

Chapter Three
My First Year

WHEN I FIRST STARTED WORKING for the library, about twelve years ago, there was no Internet. But the card catalogs were already gone, and to look a book up there was a black-and-white computer system that pulled items up by Dewey number, subject, author, and title. The people who okay'd that system were mighty proud, mighty proud, because they were librarians, not computer people, and they had gone ahead and investigated and signed off on the project and done a good thing. The computer system was self-contained, simple to learn, virtually unhackable, and laughably obsolete within six months of installation.

The few young people who were computer savvy at the library were stunned that we would bother putting in such an obviously temporary, interim system. Within the library, however, everyone was uniformly awed. A few of the really, really old-timers were absolutely aghast and against the whole thing, for reasons that have been utterly lost in time but are still cogent today. There is a horror in the new.

Another big difference between then and now has to do with union membership. When I was first hired, there was an orientation period—the one you were paid to attend—where they talked, oh, dress code, expectations of behavior, salary structure, and other arcane minutiae that would have been obvious in the first half hour of the first day at the job.

At some point in the afternoon, an earnest, rank-and-file union representative would come in and tell you all about the union: how it was a good thing, and how we should all really think about joining so that when it came time to stick it to the man, he would stay stuck. The union man was given a half hour, so he purposely stretched out his presentation to forty-five minutes just to show us how edgy he was, and when he was done he fielded questions.

The woman next to me asked a question that made all the color drain out of his face. "What if you don't want to join?"

The union official's eyes dilated, but he wiped the repugnance off of his face and answered: "Why wouldn't you want to join?" Maybe he was sincere. But he answered in an odd, grave tone—like maybe if a guy had asked that same question, he'd wade into the audience and give the guy a little smack on the side of the head and say, "What the fuck is your problem, man? You know Joe Hill died for pricks like you?"

The union man passed out a handful of green membership cards and told everyone to sign and return them by the end of his presentation. I held on to mine. I told him I was going to take it home and show it to my wife, and he understood. He was happy that I was a conscientious comrade-in-arms. So he told me, bring it back tomorrow or Wednesday and put it in the interoffice mail in care of union business, okay? No problem. And he winked at me. I did not wink back, because that would have been over the top.

I never brought the green membership card back. Eventually they made me a union member anyway, signature or not. I was called a courtesy member. It was a solidarity thing. A solid wall of vigilant, united workers against an unforgiving wall of oppressive management. It is an adorable, romantic notion that neither side seems to believe. These days there are no green membership cards, no pleading and boasting and hectoring to the new employees. You work for the city—well, congratulations, you just joined the union. You're part of us now. It doesn't take too long to figure out who the Sharks and who the Jets are. If you *are* confused, someone from the union will answer all your questions.

Management will swerve wildly from one side of the road to the other to avoid these questions. They have been warned by the city attorney not to proffer an opinion. Ask them a question about union dues and they will shake their heads and point you in the direction of a union official. As a result, the union voice is heavy, strong, and monotonous. The management side of the equation is implied. They are, however, the people who cut you a check every two weeks, and the union works hard to undercut the loyalty that a regular paycheck engenders.

The physical examination has changed drastically since the early days. Now there might be urine samples, blood tests, and questionnaires that will give the city a little backup paperwork in case you ever come down with asbestosis, tuberculosis, flesh-eating bacterial infections, or anything else you can receive from a filthy toilet seat, a befouled water fountain, or the cover of any book in the library.

The most memorable part of my physical examination consisted of coughing vigorously into my hands while a nice, older man in a white smock cradled my sack. Thankfully, there was no eye contact. I then pulled my pants back up and was asked to pick up a large wooden box filled with books, which I did. At the end of each part of the test, someone else in a white smock said "hmmm" and wrote something down on a clipboard — or at least checked something off.

The first person in the library to help me find my way around was a young Latina page named Maria. Pages occupy the bottom rung of the library hierarchy. They are paid the least, have the fewest benefits, do the most work, and are expected to move on when they finally, inevitably become dissatisfied with their lot. A library will continue to function nicely without every other position, but without the pages it would grind to a stop within a quiet afternoon. All pages are aware of this irony but are urged to keep it to themselves. No one likes a complainer.

Maria had graduated from high school, gotten married, and had a child. Her husband was a groundskeeper — he corrected me once at a casual library function and said he was *the* groundskeeper — for the Green Tree Country Club, a precious little jewel that might pay him to work there but would balk at the prospect of letting him play eighteen holes. Still, it seemed like a decent job: seeding, cutting, watering, edging, and replacing large areas with new sod. I think he felt like he was his own man.

Maria said he had gone through a few jobs because he was smarter than the people he worked for, which is in itself mundane, but her husband always found a way to throw it in their faces, which is always a bad move. Maria had a lot of faith in him, though. Someday he'd find the right job and up he'd fly like a startled bird into the rafters of management. It was just a matter of time and patience. Maria said he told her to expect these bumps in the road, because he was the kind of person to chafe under another man's rein. This was a coded message to Maria that meant she was not allowed to quit her gig at the library, or they would be staying at his parents' house for the next twenty years, raising their family in a spare room and listening to his father go to the bathroom several times a night.

Within the first month or so of my employment with the library, I was called into the senior librarian's office and given a key to the back door. This meant I could now open up first thing in the morning and close up at night. It was quite an honor. Over the next several months I'd have to figure out where the rest of the keys were stashed—and there were keys for everything.

Maria showed me which key unlocked the flagpole, which key unlocked the white bookdrop, the blue bookdrop, which set of keys unlocked the front door, and which key opened up the Xerox copier to change out the dry ink cartridges. She also knew which keys, hidden in back, unlocked the thermostat covers so you could fiddle with the temperature in the library. A forbidden, unholy thing to do but oh, so satisfying.

There were keys to supply cabinets, keys to video and cassette cases, keys to the restrooms, and keys to the towel dispensers *inside* the restrooms. There were even backup keys to every key in the building, and these keys were locked away in a box tucked away by the electrical boxes and the phone equipment. This box was also locked, and *this* key was hidden in the coatrack/umbrella area next to the refrigerator in the abysmal, almost unusable employee break room.

This attention to detail has resulted in almost no theft of paper towels or computer paper over the past several years. Serendipitously, the same procedures have helped foil larger crimes. Twice in the last ten years people have hidden in the restrooms after closing time intending to get locked in, come out after everyone else is gone, unplug a computer, hard drive, and monitor, and run batshit out the front door. But the front and back doors are locked, chained, and keyed shut. The keys are locked up, and the keys to unlock the keys are hidden in the unusable employee break room. After an hour or two of desperate roaming around the library, both times the thieves called the police from the front desk and complained that they had been locked inside a public library. Well, no thank you, they did not want to file a complaint or make a report, or even leave their names, they just wanted to go. So the police would call Juanita, the upwardly mobile senior librarian at our branch at the time, at home in the middle of the night, and she would look at the clock on her nightstand and call one of us—she said she was delegating certain responsibilities in order to empower us to succeed—and we'd drive back to the library, unlock the back door, and set them free.

On Saturday mornings, Maria and I would unload the outside bookdrops first thing in the morning. During this time, she'd relax and tell me all about her little girl, and how her husband was going to strike it rich as soon as he lost his goddamn attitude. Maria and I had become friends over the months, and she no longer felt obliged to tout the marital party line. Maria had doubts about the union, too. She was a slave with many owners, but she kept her attitude positive, not expecting to be rescued or saved but with a clear, vivid idea of what freedom would taste like.

On one memorable Saturday morning, we opened the second outdoor bookdrop and the conversation stopped. A horrible, foul smell wafted out. We peered in expecting to see a dead possum lodged in between layers of books. Nothing. We pulled the books out one at a time and put them on a table. About three-fourths of the way down into the books, I went back into the library and put on a pair of disposable plastic gloves from a large roll the library had purchased for just such unsavory occasions. We go through a box every few years.

There was a fecal-covered dildo wedged in between the books like a little toy rocket ship. I picked up the back end, gingerly, and set it between a few sheets of old newspaper. Maria moved away from the bookdrop, walked back inside, and asked for no further information. Juanita came out from her office, took one look, withered at the sight of it, and asked me to call 911 and file a police report. I took off the gloves, threw them in the trash barrel outside the building, and made the call.

A squad car came out more or less promptly, and two officers made short notes on a little yellow pad. Anyone angry at us? Uh-huh. How often did we empty the bookdrop? Uh-huh. When was the last time? Did we have security cameras outside the building? When I answered no, they scanned the outside of the building to make sure I was telling the truth.

I asked them if they needed to keep the thing as evidence and they declined graciously. No, sir. We don't need that thing sitting in the backseat the rest of the day, oh no. Best thing is, wrap it up in a whole big bunch of newspapers and toss it in the trash can in the back of your building. And no, we are not going to be dusting it for prints. Please. They looked at each other and exchanged meaningful, comic glances. The timing and execution were flawless.

I disposed of the device as instructed and wondered about the curious mind-set and anger of the person depositing such a thing. "Hey! Before we stop off for a nightcap, let's pull into the library parking lot! Won't take a sec!" Maria and I cleaned and Lysoled a bunch of books that had been in its general proximity. Juanita ordered several books pulled out of the computer system and discarded on general principle, and we buried them, along with the little toy rocket ship, in the same trash can. It reminded me of an old *Twilight Zone* episode.

On a rest break that afternoon, Maria and I spoke awkwardly about the whole incident. I thought it was a pretty vile thing to do. She agreed. Who drops off used sex toys at a night bookdrop for the library? It was a psychology I could not begin to understand.

Maria had worked at the library at this point for more than five years. She had never regaled me with stories and anecdotes of library life. With her, it was all child and husband.

"Weird shit," I said.

She agreed.

"Happens all the time," she said in a weary monotone.

I couldn't imagine what she meant.

Chapter Four
How It Used to Be

SOME TIME AFTER the toy rocket ship incident, I was called to the circulation desk to settle some inconsequential matter. A patron had fines for a ruined CD cover on his record and was angry when he learned that we expected him to pay a few bucks for it. Dealing with angry patrons is one of the things I do. I also process the books when they come in, call the patrons when their books are overdue, bill them when their fines hit a certain level, pull books out of the system when they become vile and ratty, and a variety of other tedious chores. Most of my duties are basically addition and subtraction, but when patrons are involved there is an emotional component. After palavering with the angry patron who had the ruined CD case on his record and agreeing to waive a few additional fines so he could feel good about the whole exchange, I walked past Maria, who was making happy small talk with an elderly patron in front of the new releases. The woman had nicely colored grayish hair coiffed the same way my mom used to coif her hair, and I had never seen her before. She had a five-hundred-page biography of Samuel Adams clutched tightly to her bosom, and as Maria chatted the woman gasped, "No!" "Oh my goodness!" and "Heavens!" Maria was getting some nice mileage out of the dildo incident. The woman looked ashen, like she might want to lean against something for a few minutes.

On the way back to the reference desk, I passed by the two again, and this time Maria stopped me and introduced us. The elderly woman had been the senior librarian at the branch ten years before I started. This woman had hired Maria years ago when Maria was only dreaming about marriage and children and family life. Her name was Gudrun.

Ten years earlier, when Gudrun was the senior librarian, I was the advertising manager for a nice-sized electronics company in the South Bay, being courted by advertising agencies, hiring and firing vendors, and wielding a $750K ad budget like a mighty sword. So it was several lifetimes ago.

Gudrun remembers how it used to be. She is not a big fan of change.

In the library, we have cartons of old, neglected scrapbooks that provide an informal documentation of the library's entire life, including the ribbon cutting, pictures of storytimes from twenty-five years ago, and candid shots from staff potlucks. One of the differences you notice right away is that staff luncheons used to include glasses of wine. You'd have a paper plate—not yet plastic—with salad, spaghetti, egg rolls, cubed cheese, potato chips, and an adorable little glass of white or red wine. There was enough alcohol poured to bring a faint flush to powdered cheeks, enough alcohol to recommend Dashiell Hammett or Ed McBain to someone you knew liked Raymond Chandler. That much alcohol. Not enough to turn up the music on the unobtrusive, black AM/FM radio, kick off your shoes, and dance, not enough to hit on a colleague, and certainly not enough to stumble out into the parking lot and vomit between the Mustangs and VWs. Still, it was cutting-edge audacity for the early '60s.

A single bottle of wine today would bring down the walls of the temple. Someone might have to be fired, and at the very least there would be a severe reprimand in someone's personnel file. We are bigger drinkers now, but more anxious not to appear so. Alcohol is no longer a symbol of conviviality and fellowship. In the library, drinking would be considered a measure of sedition and defiance. There would have to be punishment, and shame would be good, too.

Gudrun remembers a civic group, now long defunct, that was responsible for putting fresh flowers in the library each week on the reference desk. Simple bouquets, a spray of daisies, a few stems of roses. Fresh flowers are not hard to find in California most of the year, but that a civic group concerned itself with such a thing now seems almost unimaginable. Old school. After a few days the women librarians wore the flowers on their dresses, and it seemed to add a modicum of aristocracy to the floor of the library.

Today the dress code is more all-encompassing. Wear a dress shirt or a T-shirt, dress pants or jeans. Your hair can be purple or blonde, black or orange, and you can spike it, wear it in a mohawk, or shave it all off. After you've put in your first thirty days, there's not much they can do about it, and it might be rude and even actionable to mention it. People still bring in flowers, but rarely, maybe once or twice a year. We get more baked goods than flowers.

One of the differences that Gudrun remembers fondly is the shoe allowance that the city contributed. Every full-time employee— and that meant every *woman* employee—was given a stipend twice a year in their regular paychecks to buy durable, sensible, slightly uncomfortable black shoes. Men as a group did not work in the library, and it's still a bit of an aberration. Maybe it was a result of men being pulled into the service during World War II; maybe it's always been kind of a feminine domain. In any case, the city regularly kicked in for librarians to buy shoes.

They don't anymore.

To Gudrun these were the good old days. The library closed at six every night so everyone could go home and have dinner, there were no cell phones regularly going off like sputtering noise bombs, children were never left unattended, and the libraries were always . . . quiet. Clean. Civil. On Thanksgiving, there were hokey displays of turkeys and pilgrims and Indians, and on Christmas the YMCA donated a Christmas tree that sat in front of the reference desk and was adorned almost exclusively with children's handmade ornaments.

Now, you can put in a Christmas tree but forget trying to slip in any of this birth-of-the-baby-Jesus nonsense. Call it a religious holiday and zealots from other religions will be clamoring for equal time. Juanita even put up a cautionary memo on the bulletin board right next to the abysmal, almost unusable employee break room, that we all had to initial after reading, warning us to wish people a happy holiday, not a merry Christmas. Thank goodness Kwanzaa came along when it did—now when you wish people happy holidays, it might mean Hanukkah, Christmas, *or* Kwanzaa. You're touching all the bases, offending no one's sensibilities.

Another difference in the library now occurs during crafts. You used to use the library's crayons, drawing your mother and father, and the "flesh"-colored crayon meant you were drawing white people. If you happened to be Japanese or Chinese, you'd be using the yellow crayon, and if you were African-American you'd be using black. But no longer. The library has purchased, at an inordinate, almost government contract–like expense, something called multicultural crayons. There are a dozen of them per box, and each marker has been designed to more assiduously resemble different racial tones. It is a sincere if misguided effort, less bawdy than its predecessor.

Gudrun still comes into the library, and she still reads four to six novels a week. She misses the constant stream of new material, being the first one on the block to read a best seller, and she misses the camaraderie she once enjoyed with staff and patrons alike. One thing Gudrun has no desire to see is the stream of latchkey kids who come into the library right after school and stay until six or seven at night. Four hours a day is too much for a child, too much for most adults. Even if doing a thing is fun, do you want to keep at it for four hours a day, twenty hours a week? We are adults. We are paid to be here. It is a job—one of those real jobs I had successfully avoided for years. Four hours a day for a child in the library is close to four hours of minimally supervised hell.

When a child is dropped off for that many hours, it's free day care, pure and simple. The library is heated in the winter, air-conditioned in the summer, there are adults in charge, and there are clean restrooms. By not thinking about it too closely, or too clearly, parents think they are doing a good turn for their children. The kids get to catch up with their friends, get a leg up on their homework, and relax after a hard day of schoolwork. And that is the flawed yet attractive theory they are going with.

The kids didn't do this in Gudrun's time. They didn't have to. In those days, Mom was already at home, working on dinner, and there was someone to come home to. It felt good to be a kid and walk into a house with your mom busy doing whatever it was she did all day. But now Mom is out working somewhere, too. The kids are going home to empty houses. Dark rooms in empty houses. Parents are wary about having their kids alone in the house. Here, a parent's imagination works just fine. The boys will get bored and start wrestling in the living room, eventually rolling into an end table and knocking everything to the floor. They will throw a football inside the house and break a window, knock a vase to the floor. They will find dad's *Penthouse* and jack off. They will drink cleaning supplies and put their feet on the table and watch MTV. Then they will wander back to the *Penthouse* and jack off again. Girls will do the same thing, but differently. No, no, the library is a much better idea. Nothing bad can happen to them there.

But plenty does happen at the library, especially when you're given four hours a day to think about it. You'd think a kid doing homework from 3:30 to 6:30 every day would be cutting a dazzling, high-profile swath through school, but there's a wrinkle. We don't make them do homework. We are not their parents. We don't have a vested interest in their success. Not surprisingly, a lot of the kids dumped off at the library for three and four hours a day are the same kids who wind up taking summer school because they failed their subjects the first time around.

Maybe, their disgruntled parents think, if you have to do four hours of homework a day and still don't understand it, it's too hard.

They still don't get it.

Gudrun gets it. She comes in and browses the aisles, regularly checking her watch for the time. She is a Cinderella preparing for the witching hour. In this case, however, the witching hour coincides with the last school bell of the day, when streams of bored, wild, slightly resigned kids pour in who have been told to wait in the library until their parents pull into the parking lot and honk their horns.

Juanita has urged Gudrun to stay and watch the library fill up, watch the activity level and the noise level increase, but Gudrun declines. This is not a thing she wants to witness. To her, this would be like watching an anaconda swallow a baby rabbit. She is adamant. To Juanita, this is a sign that Gudrun has lost the eye of the tiger, she's lost her edge. She'd never make it now as a children's librarian. Too set in her ways.

Gudrun doesn't care. She wants to be done looking at books by this time. She wants to be checked out, in her car, windows rolled up, far away when the first shock waves of children hit the front door of the library. She would rather remember the library as a place of innate nobility and literacy, and she would rather remember the children in her mind the way they used to be, not the way they seem to be now.

Chapter Five
The Reference Desk

ONE OF THE REGULARS GUDRUN will go out of her way to seek out and say a quick hello to is Henry. This is kind of surprising, because Henry is an intensely reclusive patron who does not speak much. To anyone. Usually he sits by himself and glares openly if he is approached. But he is quietly gracious with Gudrun. He will even bow slightly when they shake hands and Gudrun asks coquettishly if everyone on the library staff is minding their manners. He has been coming to the same library, almost daily, for more than fifteen years, and I think Gudrun appreciates a little continuity in the place.

Henry is slender, perhaps fifty-five years old or a bit younger, mostly bald, with a salt-and-pepper mustache that he chews on when he is nervous or one of his demons is bothering him. The word from Terri, the children's librarian, is that he lives in subsidized housing somewhere nearby and walks everywhere. He has no car. He has asked at the reference desk for the *Kelley Blue Book* a few times but is stunned when he sees the price of a modest used car he thought he could afford. When his medications are off, he grows angry at himself and will have the courtesy to go outside before he starts shouting and cursing at himself. If he cannot find peace standing in the sun in front of the library, he will walk around the block a few times before he even thinks of coming back in. On particularly black days, we will see him leave the library, walk around in the parking lot, come back in briefly, realize it is not working, and leave again. If he cannot control himself, he leaves and will only come in again the next day.

He first comes in after we've been open for an hour or so, around noon. He walks in, grabs a pencil with at least a vestige of an eraser from the cup at the circulation desk, goes over to the newspapers, finds the *Los Angeles Times*, and makes himself a copy of the crossword puzzle. He works on it off and on throughout the day. Most of the time, he will work on the crossword puzzle by himself, but he will occasionally come up to Terri, when she is on the reference desk, to ask for help. Because he is not a native English speaker, he often stumbles over idioms and colloquial expressions.

One morning, he puts the crossword puzzle on the reference desk in front of her and asks for help with fourteen across. It is a five-letter answer and the clue is "unplastered." So far, he has the letters _OBER. The clue makes no sense to him whatsoever, but Terri gets it immediately.

"Sober!" she says with a quiet laugh. Henry still doesn't get it, so Terri pulls a copy of *Roget's Thesaurus* off the shelf and spends almost a half hour—well into her lunch break—showing him how to use it. "Plastered," she tells him, is a colloquialism. She says she understands why he had such a hard time with that one. Henry smiles pleasantly. It is the smile of a boulevardier. He is making casual small talk with a woman.

Occasionally, he will take the unabridged *Webster's Dictionary* to his desk. Depending on the difficulty of the crossword puzzle, he will ask for other books from the reference desk: a field guide to North American trees, an index of world poetry and poets, or an overview of Etruscan civilization, intent on breaking the back of that day's crossword puzzle.

When I first started working in the library, the after-school regulars called him the Spitter. He would be working on his crossword puzzle when the middle school across the street got out for the day, and when the kids came pouring in, loud and ripping at the seams as they almost always are, he would lash out explosively and tell them: Shut up! Why are you making such noise! Filthy horrible children! Why don't you go! Go! Go if you're going to be like this!

Library personnel would all rush to the scene like paramedics and tell the kids to be quiet, move away, find somewhere else to sit, and someone would tactfully ask Henry not to shout at the children. Best not to interact with them at all, we'd tell him. Within the first few days of that school year, the kids would figure out not to sit by that old man in the corner of the library. He shouts and spits at people! He's crazy!

More than once, I will come across Henry standing in front of the restroom, clearly agitated. He will hand me an empty toilet paper roll and say, "You're out of toilet paper!" This is an odd thing, because Mr. Weams and his custodial crew fill up the toilet paper dispenser every morning. I think perhaps Henry is stealing toilet paper. Perhaps wherever he lives, people are expected to buy their own toilet paper, and Henry is simply stretching his limited dollars.

Over the past ten years he has come in twice wearing a sports coat and a tie. The first time, Terri compliments him on the look and he looks pleased, pleased to be having a normal conversation with another person. He still just glares at me, probably because I have warned him several times about shouting at terrified little children. Terri is kind, though, and Henry confesses to her that he is going to a job interview. An architectural firm.

An architectural firm? When Terri tells us this detail later, everyone is stunned. We can't wrap our minds around it. Henry? Working? At an architectural firm? We realize we know nothing about this man.

Weeks later when Henry is experiencing one of his gregarious periods, Terri asks him about the interview. He responds only with the obvious: he didn't get the job. Terri chats with him a little more, but it is clear he does not want to talk about it. He has the crossword puzzle under his arm and he is anxious to get started. He is back to his routine. Out of sight, nicely sequestered, working on his crossword puzzle, and close enough to the reference desk to walk over if he ever needs an information fix.

It's not such a bad idea. In the library, the reference desk is where it's all at. It is the chalice, the grail, the golden fleece. In a skeletal diagram from a reference book like *Gray's Anatomy* it would be the skull, though that would be a little self-congratulatory. But it is the anchor to the whole place, ground zero in the library. Everything else is warehousing and processing and accounting, books waiting to go back out, books coming back in, books in the back with broken spines, books in piles waiting to be cataloged, and books that have been weeded and are waiting for a dark night to be tossed into the Dumpster.

If you want to, you can ignore the reference desk and drift through the stacks like the Flying Dutchman, hoping to self-navigate to just the right book. When a person finds a good book this way it is like finding money. You can grit your teeth and saddle up on the Internet and ride that wherever it takes you, or you can walk up to the reference desk and ask.

You may be dissuaded from this, because there's a good chance that the person sitting at the reference desk does not look like the kind of person you'd want to have anything to do with. It may be a mousy, feverish-looking man in an out-of-date suit or an old hippie in a Hawaiian shirt and rumpled pants. The man has lambchops, a handlebar mustache, or a beard. He is pale, out of shape, the color of meat left in the sink overnight. The woman sitting there is wearing a powerful, lilac, old-lady perfume and a brooch from another century. They are sedentary, the skin on the face and arms being pulled to the ground, the men and women both seemingly too old for their bodies. They are the polar opposite of MTV spokespersons.

There is a term librarians use called the "reference interview." The reference interview happens because the person coming up to the reference desk doesn't really have a handle on what they want. They know what they want to know, but—just like in *Jeopardy*—they have a hard time putting it in the form of a question.

"Is there an oration section?"

"An oration section? What do you mean?"

"You know. Speeches. Books about speeches."

"Like you have to give a speech and want to know how to put it together?"

"No. Like, famous speeches."

You want to whisper, Why won't you just tell me?

"Famous speeches. Any particular kind?"

"Yes. About racism."

"Okay. Speeches about racism. Throughout the world or just in this country?"

"This country. The United States."

"Recently? The last fifty years?"

"No."

"Earlier?"

"A lot earlier. Like Civil War stuff."

"Like the Lincoln-Douglas debates?"

"Yeah. But not the debates. Like, about the debates. Like, commentary. Like who they thought won."

Commentary on the Lincoln-Douglas debates. We have that. If only he knew what to ask for.

Working on the reference desk, it's not uncommon to knock one after another out of the ballpark. What is the middle of the sun made of? Are there satellite photos of Area 51? How should I construct a trebuchet? When is the next eclipse? What's my congressperson's mailing address? Where can I get a schematic diagram of a 1974 Dodge Dart engine? Why do we have leap years?

But these are questions at the easy end of the spectrum. They can get much harder. "I'm renting an apartment and I found this little dog—he had been attacked by a larger dog and I rescued him—so I took him home and he seemed to get better. This morning my landlord says he's going to evict me, because it says no pets in the lease. I told him it wasn't a pet. I was just going to take care of it until it got a little healthier."

Librarians are careful not to offer legal or personal advice. We don't know whether you can be evicted or not. The landlord might not, either. We do, however, have up-to-date books on landlord-tenant disputes and tenants' rights. If things get serious, we can supply lists of lawyers but we can't tell you if they're any good or not.

At the edges of the solar system of reference questions, there are things like this: "I came in here two or three weeks ago and was reading a book about the Korean War. About this big. Green. I can't find it today. Can you show me where it is?" We might, but it's going to take a lot of looking. The library doesn't catalog by size and color, and they're almost all rectangular.

The Internet has made reference questions a much easier proposition. A patron comes in and says he went to a World War II air show, saw the B-17, the Flying Fortress, and there were unusual markings on the tail, a big "K" on the vertical portion. What does the "K" stand for?

We go to Google, type in "FLYING FORTRESS WORLD WAR PLANE SYMBOL TAIL K." Less than two seconds later it tells us that "K" was the marking for planes that were stationed in Kimbolton Air Field in England. This could have been a weeklong search without the Internet. With the Internet, the whole thing took less than a minute.

How tall was the actor who played Matt Dillon in *Gunsmoke*? How many episodes of *Gunsmoke* were there? Didn't it start out as a half hour show and wind up an hour? What station was it on? What character got attacked by wolves and killed a whole bunch of them with his bare hands? Who wrote that one? Didn't one of them — I don't know who — put out an album?

Easy, easy stuff. Ten years ago, we would have shaken our heads and suggested the patron write to the television network. Who knows crap like this? And who wants to know? Is this a bar bet? Are you some kind of a nut? A *Gunsmoke* stalker?

So we use the Internet.

I had never used the Internet until I began working at the library. I was one of those people on a historic cusp; we didn't learn it

in school, my folks didn't have it at home, and there didn't seem to be
any reason to try a thing I had done without my entire life. When I was
in middle school, there was no such thing as classes in computer literacy, and outside of certain universities hardly such a thing as computers. The boys took a class called Wood, where you learned the value
of safety goggles and discovered a multitude of ways you could cripple
yourself for life in the quest for badly made wooden knickknacks. The
girls had their own class—Typing. I signed up for typing, not because
of any confusion over my gender but because I wanted to be a writer,
maybe a journalism student. The guidance counselor took me into
his office and asked me to reconsider. A guy in a class full of girls. He
thought it might lead to me getting picked on. I assured him that I was
already getting picked on, and the idea of more didn't bother me. He
threw up his hands in resignation and agreed.

He was not so agreeable the very next semester when I asked to
take Home Economics instead of Metal. He didn't buy my argument
that I'd need to cook for myself in the years ahead and saw my request
as some kind of sick farce. He put his foot down. Metal class it was.

Juanita was the senior librarian when the library installed its first
Internet connection. When they did, they wisely disabled the sound
cards, effectively muting the computer. But because we are the library,
we resisted the urge to filter information. It all comes through.

Within the first three weeks, I saw things I never expected to see in
the public library. Video clips of public executions and animals giving
birth in the wild. Morgue shots of celebrities. Cute, little miniature golf
courses that you could play for hours. U.S. presidents getting rouged
and powdered for their television appearance. And, oh, the porn.

Pornography on the Internet is not a hard thing to find. As a child,
I was introduced to pornography in the time-honored fashion: I crept
into my parents' bedroom when they weren't home and leafed through
one of my dad's *Playboys*. I had a good idea about what I was going to
find—beautiful young women in bathing suits throwing cheap plastic
beach balls around, rolling around on the sand, smiling and relaxed. I

opened the magazine and felt like I had walked in front of a bus. They were naked. Rolling around on a bed. Smiling and relaxed.

Frequently, a young family comes into the library with extremely young children in tow. They haven't been into the library in a while, but their memories of the place are very pleasant. They sign up for library cards, ask about the summer reading club, inquire about storytime in the mornings, and eventually they sign their children up for library cards too. We encourage it. It's something akin to a first credit card.

Of course, when a two-year-old checks out *The Poky Little Puppy* and it disappears, we have no beef with the child. Children lose stuff. They can't sign contracts. We know that. We bill the parents for *The Poky Little Puppy* and the parents are often stunned, stunned that they are legally responsible for their own children. Perhaps a small part of their minds thought the system would just absorb it, like a *Star Trek* alien slurping up great bursts of energy from the photon torpedoes. For god's sake, they're just children, the parents sputter. Maybe we shouldn't have given them library cards in the first place, if that's the way the library's going to be.

The Internet is worse.

How can the city encourage technology that is so user-friendly, so easy for a young child to use, when a few innocent mouse-clicks away there are teens only slightly older than their children, smiling, naked, glassy-eyed, legs open, there are cocks being sucked, orgasms being photographes and recorded, and genitals being prodded, displayed and manipulated—in the library? In the library.

The first time this happened, a young man with his parents was putting together a science project on which brand of diapers were the best for holding the most urine. The boy's modest plan was to get on the Internet, find the statistics, print them out, and glue them to his rather sparse diorama. His folks were so proud. They all smelled an A+ just around the corner. Soon, his mother came to the reference desk and she was clearly not well.

They had Googled "diapers" and a few other terms, and had

stumbled onto a number of lusty sites where adults wore diapers for, oh, personal satisfaction. One mind-scalding photo of a fifty-year-old man in a diaper casually holding a cocktail in a birdbath martini glass put the whole project on indefinite hold. Their child was posing questions that he hadn't the words for yet, and the parents were similarly at a loss for words. In the library? Juanita steered the lummy parents to a display of science project books, and they checked out two G-rated books on photosynthesis.

It is the Pandora's box dilemma. Knowing how limitless the Internet is, who would not want to look around a little?

Max is one of our regulars, he is an adult, and he comes into the library every weekday at around two in the afternoon and stays until eight at night. His eyes are not good, he is quiet, and he is of limited means. He is looking for a wife from South America—some handsome woman who might be happy with a nearsighted American with almost no money. Every day he goes to various Web sites, looks at photographs of attractive women, and prints out the finalists to ponder over later. He is not interested in pornography. He is lonely.

After six months of this, it was somewhat of a joke. He seemed to be going after the best damn woman in South America, maybe the entire hemisphere. After a year it wasn't funny anymore. His search had deteriorated from one desperate type of pathos to another. Buying a wife was no longer the payoff—it was the limitless possibilities of searching for one. He had stared into Pandora's box too long, too intently, and it was no longer possible to close it. He didn't want it closed.

When we shut down for the evening, we have to kick Max off the Internet. There are always a few dozen more applicants to print out. He has whittled the list of finalists down to several hundred.

It is what we call "information." You can find something about anyone.

One of the few people you will not find using the Internet is Henry. He has no driver's license, no credit cards, no cell phone number, belongs to no organizations or associations, and as far as we know has no last name. He will not use the Internet, and perhaps doesn't trust it for reasons he is not entirely comfortable talking about. He uses the reference books instead—partially to find out the name of a six-letter percussion instrument made of dried gourds and partially to say hello to Terri and ask her how her day is going.

Chapter Six
Illegal Activity

A VERY CURIOUS EVENT UNFOLDED during the first few weeks of this new school year. Early on a Tuesday morning, Cynthia—one of the morning pages—found a small scrap of paper by the front door printed with the message: THERE IS A BOMB IN THE MEN'S ROOM. The note could have been slipped through the door in the middle of the night. It could have been dropped intentionally before we closed up the night before, or a little kid could have written it as a joke during a class visit yesterday afternoon. And it did kind of look like a child's handwriting.

The library was not yet open. Cynthia gave the note to Lillian, the senior librarian at the time, who peeked inside the men's room and saw nothing. The children's librarian, Terri, suggested evacuating the building and calling the police. There are actually a few swell, not-so-hard-to-access hiding places in the public restrooms, as two convicted drug dealers proved a few years ago. There is an utterly nasty floor vent that can be unscrewed with a pocket knife, and there are ceiling panels that can be popped out with a brisk shove by anyone over five-foot-six.

Lillian did not call the police, although that seems to be clearly labeled Step One. Librarians are genetically programmed to ignore this procedure. They see it as a flaw of character, a failing of sorts, a mes-

sage to administration that they can't handle it, like a professional boxer
calling in the referee and asking for a time-out for the last minute of the
round so he can stand in the corner, sip some water, and clear his head.

The scene reminded me of something that happened during my
first year in the library. It had been raining, hard, and I looked out the
front window just in time to see a car skid, the wheels lock up, and
a student from the middle school across the street step off the curb. I
heard the dull, unimpressive *whump* as the student popped into the
air, landing a few feet away in a tangle of limbs.

Peg Peters, the almost retired, dour, and imperious children's
librarian at the time, was at the reference desk. She was just getting off
the phone and I told her that there had been an accident. I reached
for the phone and she put out a cautionary hand to block me.

Had I seen this "accident"?

Yes.

Hmm. Where?

Out the window, on the corner by the traffic light.

Hmm. Do you know if anyone's hurt?

Probably the kid who flew through the air.

She gave me the pinched, biting-into-a-lemon face to let me
know she acknowledged the dark humor but didn't approve.

But you don't know, she said.

And I looked at her like, What the fuck?

She cocked her head as if she felt vaguely sorry for me for not
understanding the ways of the world—especially the library—and
said: You should talk to Juanita before you do anything. If anyone calls
the police, it should be the senior librarian. Then she smiled her sad,
bemused smile that she saved for retarded people who are struggling
to appear normal.

So I picked up the phone and dialed 911.

Peg Peters's smile shattered into a million sharp pieces and her
head snapped back in betrayal and disgust. I had violated the time-

honored chain-of-command thing, called the police, and disobeyed a supervisor. Quite a trifecta for a recent hire.

Now, years later, with a bomb threat that may or may not be the work of a prankish child, Lillian the senior librarian (who wanted to be known as a person who could make the BIG decisions) makes the big decision, and dials library administration. While she waits on hold at the reference desk, administration calls Parks and Recreation, and Parks and Recreation wastes no time in calling the Fire Department. The Fire Department calls back library administration and suggests we bring in the Community Lead Officer from the Police Department. Library administration calls Lillian back—still waiting on another line at the reference desk—and suggests we call the police.

The Community Lead Officer is called, and he is relaxed, confident, and dubious. Nah. Probably just some kids. Anyway, it's been a few hours. Hell, it would have blown up by now. Ha ha. Probably nothing at all. Kids. What are you going to do? What we'll do, we'll go to the school over the next few days and talk to the teachers, tell them how serious this kind of thing is.

How it can lead to dozens of unnecessary phone calls.

Two years ago, the library was a brief home to two local drug dealers and, although we knew they were hinky and generally unsavory, we had no idea they were using the place as an ad hoc distribution point and warehouse for methamphetamines.

One was tall, thin, white, and eternally nervous. The other was the same age, late twenties, Latino, beefy, short, and maybe two hundred pounds heavier. They'd hang, bored, in the parking lot before we opened, look through the trash can out front, use the restroom together as soon as we opened, and read the newspaper for an hour or so afterward. Occasionally there would be incoming/outgoing phone calls on the pay phone just outside the front door.

We figured they were homeless gay guys and left it at that. The men's restroom is not big enough for two adults and privacy. Maybe one of them went in to take a crap while the other stood on the other side of the door and said droll and amusing things. If there was sex involved, it had to be cramped and unfulfilling for both parties. But it *was* the public restroom, not the employee restroom. The janitors came in every morning and lit up the restrooms with a barrage of bleach and chemicals, if not for the sake of the drug dealers then for the dozens of other people who used it after they did every day.

One morning, two South Bay policemen walked into the library, wandered around until they found the two guys reading the funnies, and asked politely if they wouldn't mind going outside for a little talk. Why no, they wouldn't mind. What's the problem, officers? The officers smiled and said, Hey, no problem at all, let's just go outside.

As soon as they reached the door, the tall, thin one put his head down and went into a dead run. The short fat Latino tried to follow his lead but his body resisted him. The police did not give chase. They called it in on the police radio and saturated the area with patrol cars. The fat guy was sitting on the curb less than a block away, taking in large gulps of air, all the gazelle burned out of him. The police car pulled up, the short, fat guy stood up, and before they were out of their car his hands were behind him, ready for the cuffs. The tall, thin one ran for several more blocks, went into a private driveway, and hid underneath a car. Twenty minutes later he crawled out, walked nonchalantly back onto the street, and was immediately arrested by the police who were sitting in their cars waiting for him to come out from wherever he had been hiding.

Here's what the cops told us.

The two were drug dealers, and they brought the drugs into the library and kept them there, stashed behind the vent in the men's restroom. Someone would call on the pay phone and tell them what they wanted. One of the guys had an old, ratty green backpack that they threw into the trash can out front. They'd go inside, retrieve the drugs from the restroom, catch up on the newspapers for a while, then go back outside to check on the green backpack, which by this time had accrued a nice chunk of cash. Take out the cash, put in the drugs. End of transaction. Everyone's happy.

The whole event was quite a shocker, but not as shocking as when the same two guys came back into the library two days later. Bailed out and free once more, they were trying to pick up where they left off before the police had interrupted them. Juanita called the police and asked them if this was usual. It was, at the very least, awkward.

They sent the same two policemen who again cordially asked to speak to them outside. This time the men bridled. The tall, thin man said they were just using the library. They were citizens after all. They had, you know, rights.

Or so they assumed.

One of the policemen disagreed.

"You can never come to this library again," he told them. He put up his hand. "Don't argue with me. You just can't. Not to read the newspaper, not to use the pay phone, nothing. If it's raining, say, and you're walking past—you can't come in to get out of the rain. You blew it. Come in again and the librarians are going to call us and we're going to come and, you know, take you away."

"Arrest us?" the tall, thin one asked.

The patrolman smiled grimly. "No. Just take you. Somewhere else."

The two left.

One of the two patrolmen returned about a week later to explain something. When the tall, thin guy took off, the reason he ran was because he was holding drugs. He had to get rid of them. When they caught him he was clean. They searched the area until they found a handful of hypodermic needles stashed in a nearby children's sandbox. A kid playing with that stuff would have died. The policemen—all of them—didn't like the two much, and for that one simple reason. Most of the patrolmen had kids.

Shortly after that, we called the phone company and changed the phone outside the front door so that it would no longer accept incoming calls. Outgoing calls only. Since then, we have seen a few entrepreneurs try to set up shop using the pay phone outside the library. It takes them about half a day to realize that no one is calling them back. Their efforts wither and die, they file for bankruptcy, and they move on.

The next time the police are summoned, it is spring of the following year. It is a bright, cool morning in February, and young Ms. Castro and her third graders have walked to the library from the elementary school for a field trip. The kids are lined up at the front door, excited, and a few are holding hands. We let them in before the library opens, let them wander through the library with no other patrons around to make them shy, and Terri makes a special presentation with a few songs, stories, some show-and-tell, a little sock-puppet play. The program may not sound like a winner on paper but it always brings the house down. Third graders are easy like that. Ask them to sing and they'll sing. Ask them to listen and the majority will listen. Ask them to close their eyes and think of something, they'll close their eyes and think of that thing. They're ready to have fun, and if you're advertising a good time they're ready to buy.

When a class walks to the library, it's usually the teacher in front, some alpha students right behind them trying to overachieve, and a few parent volunteers way in back to shepherd the strays and stragglers. Standing in front of the library, the teacher raps on the glass door and the kids are advised to stay in line, stay in twos, while one of the parents quickly volunteers to make a head count, ensuring that nearby lakes and ponds will not have to be dredged later in the day.

The front door is unlocked and the kids stream in, in some small way awed that a large public building has been opened just for them.

Ms. Castro, however, looks concerned.

Immediately, she pulls Juanita aside. She says there is a man outside, sitting in a wheelchair in a blind spot to the front door, and he seems . . . drunk! Actually two men, him and a friend. The man in the wheelchair is dressed as a dancer, too, a ballet dancer. There is much about both of them that troubles her.

I agree to walk to the outside bookdrop, deposit a book, and check them out as I walk back inside. The move is an obvious ploy, but what do I care? If a man dressed as the male lead from *Swan Lake* springs from the shadows and begins to maul me, my coworkers know enough to call the police.

When I come back inside I shake my head.

Juanita asks, "It there a guy dressed like a dancer?"

"Yes," I say.

"Really?"

"Well, not altogether," I have to admit. "Mostly just the colorful spandex tights and the little tutu."

"Oh, well then. And drinking?"

"They're sharing a fifth of whiskey. And there are some beer cans."

Juanita grimaces, making a face like she's just taken a big gulp of their warm whiskey. "Call the police," she says. "And wait by the front door."

The police come in the twinkling of an eye, and that's what you have to love about this town. The houses may be overpriced but a lot of the cops actually live around here. Their children are in the schools. A drunk menacing third graders at a public library? Ain't gonna happen. Not here. The police car pulls into the parking lot, they take one long look at the pair, and call for backup even before they get out of the car.

The man pushing the wheelchair is in his late twenties, wearing a Hawaiian shirt, filthy old jeans, and drunker than you'd want a person to be who is pushing another person in a wheelchair at 9:15 in the morning. The man in the wheelchair is also drunk and wearing a tutu and brightly colored, striped leg warmers. The stripes are very thinning.

One of the police officers takes the half-empty whiskey bottle and dumps it into the street. He asks the man in the wheelchair why he is wearing a tutu and leg warmers. The man in the wheelchair answers that it is because the day is so warm. The policeman nods and takes out a pencil.

The interrogation is brief. The whiskey has burned off their decorum and they are a little outraged. They, too, are familiar with their rights.

Isn't he allowed to wear a tutu?

Oh, he absolutely is.

Leg warmers?

Yes, absolutely.

What they aren't allowed to do is lurk in the parking lot of a public library where little kids have to see them. Neither of the policemen wants to arrest them, nor do they want the two in the backseat of their patrol car. The paperwork would not be commensurate with the offense. Drunk and impersonating a soloist. So they tell the pair they are going to leave and return in fifteen minutes. If they are still there, *then* they'll be arrested.

"What about my whiskey?" the man in the tutu and leg warmers growls at the two armed officers. You had to admire the moxie. He had visions of being reimbursed.

"Yeah," one of the policemen says as he puts his pencil away. And then he gives the two drunks a look that sobers them up right away. "Fifteen minutes," he says. "Awright, guys?"

"Ahhhh," they answer.

In five minutes they are gone.

Ms. Castro's class lines up by the front door and Terri gives each one a psychedelic sticker from a large pad as they leave. The kids think this is great. I walk outside before the class does to make sure the drunks are completely gone.

Ms. Castro leads them down the street, heading back to the classroom. It is very pleasant to see a class of third graders walking down the street, going back to their school in the cool of a February morning.

"Like *Make Way for Ducklings*," Juanita says in a soft voice to Terri.

Terri agrees. Without the two drunks it was a very pretty picture.

Chapter Seven
The Civil Servant's Cycle of Life

A CIVIL SERVANT LIVES in a strange and wonderful land, where the normal rules and bylaws of employment and commerce do not hold true. A civil servant cannot be promoted for doing exemplary work, nor can he be fired for doing shoddy work. Discover a cure for cancer or pull a public official out of a burning office building, and it will not get you a promotion, an enhanced title, or a salary increase. The same is true at the other end of the spectrum. Clip your toenails at the reference desk or watch home videos on the Internet when you are sitting at the circulation desk, and you might get a snippy note in your personnel file, or a "below average" box checked off at your next annual performance review, but they're still going to cut you a paycheck every fourteen days.

This means that employees are expected to find their own motivation. It also means that, not finding this motivation, an employee will occasionally go bad. There are workshops, seminars, computer classes, brown-bag lunch meetings, memos, handouts, and even weekend retreats on the subject of how to keep an employee from going bad. They have the peppiest of titles: "Harassment in the Workplace," "Recognizing Stress," "How to Deal With Problem Patrons," "Options for Your Retirement Package," and so on, but despite the appearance

of diversity these courses are really about only one thing: keeping employees from going bad.

The library does not want its employees to go bad, and for good
reason. They're civil servants. They're literally impossible to get rid of.
An employee who burns out and becomes a bad apple at the age of
thirty can fester and stink up the place for the next twenty-five years.
This happens with enough regularity to be a real concern, perhaps *the*
real concern.

Mr. Weams, the head of the janitorial crew that sweeps through
our library every morning, has worked for the city for twenty-two years
and is close enough to retirement that it is all he thinks about. He is
black, lives in South Central Los Angeles, and does not like to start
talking about the people he cleans up after in the library. Mostly it's
because, when he starts, it is too easy to continue and so hard to stop.
He becomes an out-of-control, eighteen-wheeler on an icy downhill
turnpike. No brakes, no control. In brief, he thinks that all white people are crazy, and that the white people in Bay City are the craziest.
The way they dress, the things they say, the cars they drive, even the
way they put out their trash in the morning. Crazy!

Mr. Weams may sound like a cliché from a sitcom that has been
off the air for decades, but I think he absolutely knows what he's doing,
that it is all a careful pose. I believe that at this point in his life he does
not want to be known as an articulate black man with a sizable chip on
his shoulder. I think that he is more comfortable if people just think of
him as an angry, Saturday-morning cartoon, and that it is easier to disre-
gard what he says, and easier for him to fly, almost invisibly, underneath
the radar. It makes his remaining time as a civil servant more pleasant
and peaceful. Not being taken seriously has its rewards.

Mr. Weams has modest dreams, and he lives a modest life. He
has a dog. He is unmarried. He is active in his church. He claims the
females in his church would love to find him a woman, and would do
so at the drop of a hat if he ever gave them the signal. He would like to
get out of Los Angeles when he retires and go back to coastal Georgia,

where his people are from. Land is a lot cheaper there than it is in Southern California. He would live like a prince—buy a few wooded acres, let his dog roam the property and pick up occasional ticks, and fish for largemouth bass from his own pond, his own rowboat. His dreams are very specific.

"Smallmouth bass are supposed to be fun, too," I tell him.

He shakes his head sadly, and I can tell he is sorry I am so misinformed. "What am I going to do with a bunch of smallmouth bass? You ever fish for smallmouth bass? Take you forever to get a string. And then what? Little bitty fishes ain't gonna fill a man. One nice largemouth bass, you got yourself a dinner." I get the impression he would also keep a twenty-gauge shotgun filled with double-ought buckshot behind the front door in case any crazy white folk came to visit. I tell him that I will call first.

Mr. Weams's tips on working for the civil service are brief. He says: Come to work most every day. Wear shoes and socks so they don't think you've lost your mind, and try to get along. It's not that difficult, he says. You wake up in the morning, clean yourself up, put on your go-to-work shoes, show up, go home, and do the same thing for the rest of your working life.

Listen good, he says. Don't be stupid. City ain't going to fire you for mopping the wrong way, for chewing gum during a crew meeting and popping it, for disagreeing with your boss. No sir. Ain't going to fire you for doing a bad job. If they did, hell, half the city would be out on their ass. No. Tell a dirty joke in front of a woman employee who don't want to hear it, you get written up and have to watch a film on sexual harassment. Most everyone on my crew has seen this film. Only one good reason to fire a person, and that is if the employee refuses to come to work. Hell, eventually, you got to let the person go. And who's that stupid?

The answer to this one comes from a member of Mr. Weams's own janitorial crew. He is one of the youngsters, named Russell, and Russell has been begging to be fired for three years. Russell is a redneck, a young white boy with thinning hair, an acne-scarred face, and a John Deere cap. He seems to be perpetually under the influence of mind-altering drugs. He is a heavy smoker and will stop vacuuming in the middle of a room to stand outside and have a smoke. He will leave the vacuum on, and when he does this, if Mr. Weams tells him to turn the damn thing off before he goes out, Russell will threaten to file a grievance with the union. Mr. Weams knows that sooner or later there are going to be problems. He does not want his approaching retirement dream to be fucked with in this way.

One day in the branch while the rest of us are setting up the cash and discharging the previous night's books from the bookdrop, Mr. Weams tells Russell and the others to carry the carpet-cleaning machine to the van. Russell laughs and says no way. He points to his back. He says he hurt himself over the weekend. The other janitors don't say a word, but they know that this means picking up Russell's slack. The other two janitors say a few things to each other in Spanish, laugh, and shake their heads in shared misery. It is apparent they are not crazy about the white boy either.

Russell is out for a month with this bad back. He comes back for three days and takes off again. This time he is out for six weeks. Then he is back again, no problem, the back is fine, and he talks about transferring to another department, and when that doesn't seem to pan out he begins to talk about legal remedy. They shouldn't have him lifting and carrying things when they *know* he's got a bad back.

It is one week before Christmas. Mr. Weams says he can't imagine how Russell will be buying anyone *anything* for Christmas. He works, at most, one day out of five, more likely one out of ten. Sometimes he shows up in the morning and leaves before noon. He has no sick leave left in his account. Over the past four months he has logged fewer than two full weeks. Christmas presents? Hell, how can he afford cigarettes and enough gasoline to get his truck to work? Russell tells us his plans for Christmas and New Year's. He is going to get really drunk. He's got several bottles of scotch at home all picked out. If the authorities come to harass him—as he thinks they might—they'd better know up front that he has a number of automatic weapons, and he will be sighting in on them from a position on the roof.

Oh yeah.

Mr. Weams shakes his head sadly. He tells me later that Russell has brought in some KKK literature and left it in one of the city vans. What kind of ignorant cracker lets his black superior know about his KKK leanings? Mr. Weams tells me that this is a cry for help, and that Russell is the stupidest white boy on the planet. This all fits in with Mr. Weams's worldview on white people. Russell is just the poster boy. He says you would have to look long and hard to find a black child that ignorant. He believes a black child that stupid would never have survived as long as Russell has.

The next spring, Russell turns over a new leaf. No more racist nonsense, no more bragging about the Nazi memorabilia he orders online, no more scary talk about rooms filled with automatic weapons and electronic equipment. He tells us that his girlfriend wants to start a family, and as far as she is concerned this is his last chance. She may have even thrown away his military fatigues, because he comes to the library in jeans and plain white T-shirts now. Mr. Weams keeps an eye on him. He thinks that some combination of pharmaceuticals is keeping Russell prudent and chaste, and that one day Russell will be running late and just forget to take his medications. By the end of his shift, he will be checking the bottom of the van for tracking devices and looking for unmarked cars in the rearview mirror of the city van.

By midsummer, this prediction bears fruit. Russell comes to work flushed and anxious, smelling vaguely of tropical fruit. I ask Mr. Weams if he thinks Russell is drunk. He's into something, Mr. Weams answers in a quiet voice. He is waiting for Russell's other shoe to drop. Soon after, Russell disappears from work for six weeks. He has called in with a serious back complaint and says he can barely move from the sofa. He may or may not pursue legal remedies with his employer. It's up in the air. He's talking to a few people. Lawyers mostly. He says they're waiving the $250 an hour they usually charge because the case is such a slam-dunk winner.

By fall there are no more new Russell stories from Mr. Weams. Russell has stopped coming to work completely, and no one has heard from him. The city schedules a meeting with Russell about his absen-teeism and continued employment with the city. Russell doesn't show up for the meeting. The city breathes a sigh of relief and Russell is finally let go.

Mr. Weams gets a new warm body for his crew and he can be-gin to refocus his concentration on affordable real estate in coastal Georgia. He is not surprised that Russell was let go, and not surprised at all about the length of time it took for the city to act on this bad ap-ple. Bunch of white people in committees, he says, shaking his head. Lordy, lordy, lordy.

His newest warm body lasts eight weeks and is dismissed for smok-ing a joint in an outside court at the police station, where dozens of officers on the other side of the tinted windows shake their heads at the stupid motherfucker until one of the sergeants is so embarrassed and mortified he and someone else walk outside and write the son-of-a-bitch a ticket. Mr. Weams finds out about the ticket and it is all over.

The warm body after that gets into a shouting match with Mr. Weams that is thankfully within the three-month probationary period of his employment, and he is cut loose at the end of the day. The city keeps providing Mr. Weams with fresh, warm bodies until one of them makes it all the way through this probationary period, and that is that.

Chapter Eight
A Library Page

THE PROCEDURES FOR INTERVIEWING and hiring new library personnel, especially pages, are notoriously slipshod. The questions administrators really want to ask, they cannot ask, by law. "So, that tattoo on your forehead, that means you've been in prison, right? What was the rap?" The questions they do ask have been hammered together ahead of time by a committee of like-thinking people, and under the banner of fairness they are asked of every single applicant, whether it makes sense or not. You are hiring a nineteen-year-old with little or no work experience. If there is work experience, it is uniformly unimpressive: a stint at the sub shop; delivering pizzas; working under the table at an aunt or uncle's print shop stapling newsletters together. Asking this person for a résumé is madness.

As an interviewer, what do you think you are going to hear? They come in one after the other and say they are going to work very hard and come to work every day, because that is the kind of thing administration is accustomed to hearing. They are not going to break down and come clean on shoddy work habits, problems with personal hygiene, beating up old girlfriends, former addictions, or an inability to roll out of bed every morning at the same time. No, during the employment interview, the applicants are uniformly bright, easygoing, and cheerful. Even the dark and broody ones will seem like Maria von

Trapp on the first interview. Perhaps they will be like that after you hire them. But, more likely, not.

I've invented a little game. During round one of the employee interviews, I casually walk past the windowed room where the interviews are going on and take a quick glance. By the time the fourth candidate has been interviewed I've walked by four times. At this point, I believe I have a lock on who will be chosen for the job. I have been so successful using this system that no other library employees will bet against me. I know my criteria are howlingly unfair—judging a candidate for gainful employment on the sole basis of a two-second walk-by and a casual glance at the back of his or her head. But it seems to work.

About five years ago I nailed yet another one. The first interviewee, a young woman, hadn't lasted five minutes. Her engine stalled after the initial introductions and she had nothing to say, no comments to make. She was a young Asian girl, and perhaps what she gauged as courteous and sensible workplace propriety was actually construed as a lack of personality and intelligence. The city realizes there is a time and place for vocal interaction with the public: "Stop tearing up those magazines!" or "Put the gas can down!" The city doesn't expect the person to spring into action, bowl a person to their knees, grab a fire extinguisher, or knock a bloody ax from a patron's hands, but it is a valuable thing that a person at least be able to vocalize their concern.

The second candidate came in promptly, early even, wearing a pleasant, puppy-dog face and a ripped T-shirt. The ripped T-shirt seemed less an indication of despair and economic hardship and more a statement of youthful exuberance and rebellion. So he was out. If they refuse to clean up for the interview, they certainly won't improve later in the game where there's less incentive. At the interview, they're at their best, whatever their best is. The city knows it, and anyone with a second-grade education knows it. It is impossible to be disappointed with someone who was the best he could be at the interview and was not somehow better at a later date.

The third girl was a young Latina, unremarkable, and would have been an utter shoo-in if it hadn't been for the final interview of the day: a young, Middle Eastern woman in her early twenties, wearing a burka. It would have been a close decision, but the city is all about the ethnic diversity thing so the Islamic girl was hired as the new page.

Her name was Zhila, and that's all I got to know about her then, because when Juanita took her around and introduced her, she said not a word and declined my handshake. I was later informed by an assistant librarian (who had been to a diversity seminar) that it was wholly a cultural thing. No male–female handshakes. That kind of casual pressing together of flesh could only result in smoldering lust. But even after I was informed of this, I didn't think she had a real handle on the American male ego and the lengths a male will go to fantasize.

For example, phone sex. There's very little contact going on there, and it's a billion-dollar industry. "Oh yeah — I wish I were there right now! What are *you* wearing?" That's pretty much all it takes for a guy. A plain, rough burka is not exactly the topless, towered walls of Troy. Men are pigs, I think we all know this by now. That's why sexual harassment offenders have to sit in a room by themselves and watch the forty-five-minute instructional video as punishment. A few employees have watched it twice.

Zhila was quiet. She came to work every day, she shelved books, she worked on the checkout desk, but she never engaged a male in any kind of casual conversation. She would not banter. She did not come in on Monday and talk about the crazy party she went to on Saturday night. Everyone respected that.

I assumed that she was the product of a rigorous, strenuous, assiduous, painstaking, nut-busting, religious upbringing, so I kept my conversations with her down to a haiku-like minimum. I thought god would have wanted it that way, both hers and mine. Zhila stayed that way, two-dimensional and less interesting than generic vanilla ice cream, until the afternoon of the day she was fired.

The problem began one day with the after-school rush, as so many things do. Zhila was on the checkout desk in front of the library, and the rest of us were stationed throughout the library, braced to withstand the inevitable. Terri was manning the reference desk, holding court with a dozen of her young fans, talking about new puppies, dead goldfish, yucky boys, and awful teachers who doled out too much homework. Juanita, the senior librarian at the time, was doing administrative triage inside the front door as the kids poured in. "Please, put the food in your backpack or take it outside. Please, no water bottles. There's a water fountain right next to the reference desk. Put the football away or we'll hold it for a parent to pick up. Please, put the gum back in your mouth—or do us a favor and throw it away. Let's keep the noise down to a minimum. Someone might be trying to study. Four to a table. Please. No running. Why are you licking his arm?" I was the dark and terrible thundercloud roaming through the library, ominous and threatening. As the only male employee above the page level, I was the official library Hammer. I am impervious to pleading, weeping, and the gnashing of teeth.

A flotilla of seventh-grade boys steamed into the front door who did not seem particularly bent on mischief. They were engaged in typically goofy seventh-grade conversation, and it all had something to do with MTV, Nelly, rap, and Eminem. The kids were posturing, bad, bad gangstas of the worst kind, reciting rap lyrics heavy with anger, rebellion, cops getting shot, bitches getting slapped, and all sorts of motherfuckers getting what they deserved. The words that came out of their mouths were not meant for Zhila's ears, but she heard them anyway.

Sure, I would have thrown the boys out. Freedom of speech as I interpret it gives the boys the right to hear these lyrics, but not the right to pass them on to everyone else in the library, especially seventy-year-old women who would like to think these boys remind them somehow of their grandsons. But Zhila went to the dark side before the boys could be expelled. Instead of calling for help, she found her voice and did it herself.

Her eyes dilated. Her face flushed. It was obvious no one in her family had ever said a similar thing. I imagine there had been decorum and civility in her home, and undoubtedly no MTV. The words seemed to sting her like evil rap bees. She blew her top, and I do not believe this particular top had ever been blown before. It was an event long overdue. She could have been an hour-long *National Geographic* special all by herself.

She screamed at them, and the seventh graders froze in bewilderment.

"Out! Get out! You horrible boys, horrible little sons-of-bitches! You motherfuckers! Out of the library! Out now!"

The seventh graders went into a kind of shock. Did a librarian just dive at them out of the sun, calling them motherfuckers and horrible sons-of-bitches? It seemed so. They did not immediately equate the outburst to their recitation of a rap song. School had ended, they crossed the street, walked into a library, and some kind of wild shit hit the fan, like some foul-mouthed songbird flying into a freshly Windexed plate glass window. They did not even argue. They just backpedaled out of the library.

Zhila came out from behind the checkout counter and followed them outside. After a lifetime of propriety, some internal earthen dam had collapsed. She began to cry and sob. Motherfuckers! Little goddamn bitches! It would have been quite a breathtaking thing had it happened in $200-an-hour therapy, but it was quite another thing in a crowded library.

As for the middle-schoolers, they had all heard the words before, but it was unlike any song they had ever listened to. Hey, they call each other motherfucker all day long, it doesn't mean anything. And sons-of-bitches? It was so outdated, so embarrassingly déclassé. Who is a son-of-a-bitch anymore? Pricks and cocksuckers, sure, that was the way to go, but sons-of-bitches? The names were so old school, so sixties. It was her anger and her vehemence that backed them up and frightened them. They went outside more than a little stunned.

Other library employees were there for the outburst. Juanita was up front helping a patron on the computers. One of the new pages was behind the checkout desk. I was halfway back to the reference desk, directing an older patron to the large-print books and suggesting a slightly different time of day for her next visit. We all wound up writing incident reports. Soon enough, the boys outside the library came to their senses.

Hey! Librarians aren't allowed to do that!

They're allowed to shush you, or give you a look that meant you were in serious trouble, mister, or they could waggle an ineffectual finger and threaten to call the school if you kept up the shenanigans, but call you a motherfucker? No sir. No. That was just wrong. Cursing, threatening, perhaps violent librarians. It was a concept that they could not get their minds around. Their whole world fell to pieces and not one of the subjects they took at school gave them a clue about putting it back together. Had they Googled it, it still wouldn't have helped them.

Juanita saw her world falling into pieces, too. Zhila's meltdown could have put an end to both of their careers if Juanita had handled it improperly. Juanita was an ambitious young woman, and each step in the arc of her career was a small, graceful, measured step. Up. There's nothing like a lawsuit against the city to put an end to this graceful arc.

She dragged Zhila back to the break room, handed her a box of tissues, and told her to sit, take some time, take deep, slow breaths, and compose herself. Then she went back outside to confront the boys. She told them that there was plenty of trouble to go around and, although she could take care of the situation as it stood, if parents started calling the city manager's office, she would have to explain—to the parents and the city, to school counselors and whoever else wanted to know—what had precipitated the whole mess. Eminem. Rap lyrics. Cops being shot and whatnot. Oh, my. Mother-fucker this and mother-fucker that. She was smiling now, and it was not a happy, nurturing smile.

Oh yeah.

She shook her head and smiled at them like she had every answer in the world.

The boys got the drift.

However, when Juanita went back to the break room to console Zhila and help her put together her incident report, Zhila was gone, nowhere to be found. Instead of staying put and composing herself, she had gone out the back door and driven home.

Later that afternoon, Zhila's mother and father came into the library, quietly and unannounced, and demanded a private audience with Juanita. The first thing they did was put a small tape recorder on the desk next to Juanita's statue of Dr. Seuss and asked if it would be all right to tape the conversation. The parents—the father actually, as he did all the talking—hinted at a lawsuit against the city for creating a hostile work environment. You could hear him blustering right through the closed door—especially if you were listening.

Threatening Juanita was a bad move. She had started her career in South Central Los Angeles, and then worked in Lennox, another iffy part of Los Angeles. In Lennox, they kept a baseball bat behind the checkout desk, and in South Central, a drunken homeless man tried to punch her in the face for daring to enforce the overdue book policy. Juanita was no pushover. She smiled at Zhila's parents, opened the door to her office, and declared the meeting over. Zhila was no eleven-year-old. Legally, she was an adult, albeit a hothouse variety, and Juanita would not palaver with representatives.

By ten o'clock the next morning the finished incident reports were written, rewritten until they were smooth and seamless, and faxed over to the city attorney's office for fine-tuning. Once again, Zhila's parents called, now begging for understanding, and Juanita was sympathetic and understanding in a way that would in no way tip the city's hand or convey any unnecessary information.

Zhila began calling Terri, who was at that time the assistant librarian. Terri had hired Zhila, trained her, introduced her to people, counseled her, and helped her fill out the rafts of new employee paperwork. But Terri also got the impression that Zhila was tape-recording their conversations on the phone. Once she was waiting for Terri in the parking lot after work, and after a short conversation in which Zhila asked for help and guidance she began to weep. Terri eventually went home drained, ate nothing for dinner, and felt like throwing up. Looking back, the mousy little Latina girl from the initial job interview was looking better and better, as was the obsequious, almost mute Asian girl.

A month went by and an unbelievable amount of documentation was produced. Zhila was dropped from the payroll. There was another round of page interviews and this time they went for the computer-literate punk with the bleached-blond Mohawk. Looking down the road, they knew problems would arise with the new kid, but nothing that involved outraged first-generation parents, lawsuits, and hysterical weeping. His appearance initially fueled the speculation that drug use might come into the picture, excessive absenteeism, or petty theft from the cash drawer, but that was so doable next to the three-act Greek drama of Zhila.

The bleached-blond punk with the Mohawk was named Vic, and he worked out fine. He was an anarchist, a Maoist, and a communist who liked to talk about the inevitable fall of Western Civilization and the blood in the streets to come. He was a "white hat" hacker—an ethical wiz at computer technology, rather than a pirate—who one day announced magnanimously that he had absolutely no plans to wreak havoc on the city's Web site, even though he had access to "root." Only white hat hackers could be counted on for such noble behavior and good manners. He was in a thrash band, could speak cheerfully to the elderly, and ate no meat, no milk, no cheese, no meat by-products, and no chemicals if he could help it. But if you did, hey, that was fine with him, too. He wore a seasoned, safety-pinned, painted denim jacket that he later sold for a ton of money on eBay, and he was so embarrassed with the net dollar figure that he gave the whole amount to a radical group that prepared hot lunches for the city's homeless.

Money didn't mean that much to Vic, so making shabby, unlivable wages working for the city should have kept him happy forever, but it didn't. One day he got a job working for a Korean entrepreneur in an industrial loft downtown tending to a bank of state-of-the-art computer servers, working the graveyard shift. Not only did the man offer Vic a larger paycheck, he also offered him unlimited access, whether he knew it or not, to powerful computers and powerful servers. And the page position opened up again.

Eighteen months later, Zhila came into the main branch of the library while I was behind the circulation desk. I recognized her voice and the only part of herself she had ever shown before—her face. She wore expensive jeans and had an ivory-colored silk blouse with puffy sleeves that was worth whatever she paid for it. She carried a large stack of books that were mostly feminist in nature. She glanced at me for a moment and I did not make eye contact. I scanned each of her books with the bar code reader and told her they were all due in three weeks.

Thank you, she said civilly.

You are so welcome, I said affably.

I didn't let on that I recognized her, and she didn't let on that she recognized me. Everyone was much happier that way.

Chapter Nine
The Parent Conference

I AM THE NON-NURTURING LIBRARIAN. It's the role I was born to play.

The other librarians at my branch do not have children. Juanita plans to have them someday, when she is at a point in her life where she can take a year's leave of absence. Her parents are already pressuring her. She is their only child, so she is the only possible source of grandchildren. Their schedule is empty, and has been for years, so anytime soon would be good for them. Grandma in particular would like to start the ball rolling—shopping for colorful above-the crib mobiles and cute jammies—but Juanita is not ready. Not now. She is a field marshal with her career, and now would be a mistake. This has created what appears to be a certain tension between Juanita and her mother, a tension that only a fat little baby or two will dispel.

Terri's plans for the future do not include children, although this admission is almost always met with the protestation by anyone who knows her that she would make an excellent mother. But she shakes her head, no. She does not think she would be up to the many responsibilities. Her own childhood was not particularly happy, though she will not be going into that, thank you. She is married and has a few cats, a small dog, birds, some fish. It is enough.

I have three children, and I do not agree with Juanita and Terri that the key to raising kids is understanding, listening to their problems, and speaking to them as peers, not as authority figures. This to me is lunacy. We *are* authority figures. I do not want to fall in the trap of caring if I am liked by fourteen-year-olds. This is further madness. So when one of the junior-high students peeks into the back room and sees me eating a sandwich and sipping a can of soda, I am not crushed by his accusation that there is a double standard about eating in the library. It is a double standard. I work at the library eight hours a day. I get to eat and drink in certain areas. They come in here after school, and we don't let them break out the cool ranch Doritos and the icy purple Gatorade. But I tell them this double standard thing usually works to their advantage. They are routinely getting away with stuff for which, if they were adults, they would be disciplined, imprisoned, or held and watched for seventy-two hours in specially built rooms with two-inch-thick glass. They are at the age where they have a number of built-in, get-out-of-jail-free cards.

We expect them to be rude, oafish, loud, inconsiderate, devious, and two-faced. It is part of youth, part of the steep and treacherous road to growing up. Someday they will outgrow their youth and wind up being lawyers and doctors and airline pilots and presidents of large companies. Someday they will help the helpless and give of themselves to those less fortunate. But that time is not yet.

The first time I approach an unruly group at the beginning of the school year I tell them to knock it off. Many times that's all it takes, one ominous warning from the ghost of Christmas Past. By the second or third time I tell the same group to hold down the noise, I up the ante. I tell them, look, you don't have to be here. It's not a requirement. If you want to be somewhere else, be somewhere else. If you want to be here, rein it in. Look around you. There are people trying to read books. It's a library. We are trying to encourage these people.

If I have to speak to the same group again, it means that the situation has become adversarial. Now I tell them this: We are undermanned in the library. At most, there are four of us walking around, and there may be more than a hundred students. It is not our duty, nor our desire, to walk around shushing people every five minutes, acting like every cartoon of a librarian ever drawn. Only six-year-olds get to act like six-year-olds. None of you are six. The next time I have to speak to you, I'm going to ask you to leave.

The next time I speak to them I ask them to leave.

Over the ten months of a school year, getting booted out of a public library loses its cachet. They begin to expect it. If they are clever, they can time it so they are kicked out of the library five minutes before their ride pulls into the parking lot. There has to be a next step.

The next step is the parent conference. We toss them out and bar them from setting foot back into the library until a parent or legal guardian comes in to hear the details. It's not such a big deal. Their child has done nothing horrible. But many librarians are afraid of meeting the parents. While some parents are aghast that their children have been acting up in the library, others are stunned that it's even possible to compel a child to leave a public place. How can that be? This is a public library. Can you do that? Oh, I don't think so. Spell your last name for me.

Asking to speak to a child's parent is always a good, pro-active choice, but it can be the kind of good idea that goes bad faster than you can imagine. What if the parent comes in and accuses you of throwing his child out on the basis of skin color? What if the child is already something of a god or goddess in the family? What if the child begins to sniffle and tell the parent that it was actually, sadly, the child next to him that made all the loud noises, not him?

Take Lupe for example.

Lupe was a young Filipino who threw a chair at me a few years ago when I asked him to leave for numerous infractions of the noise rule. The chair was a heavy, industrial, wooden chair made to last a thousand years that caught my right shin on the bounce. Lupe had movie-star good looks, curly black hair, and liquid brown eyes that welled with tears when I told his father the story. His father was small, goat-like in appearance, gaunt from years of grinding overtime, and nowhere near as attractive as his son.

Lupe's father suggested that the problem might have something to do with his son's perception that I didn't like him. I heard this suggestion and glanced at Lupe. The liquid eyes, the puffy lips, the pink indignation. Of course I didn't like him. His son had thrown a large chair at me. It could have broken a bone, opened the skin, ruptured aqueous humor. He stood, weepy, in front of an enraged father who wanted to know if I liked his son. What was there to like?

Two years ago, we had another parent conference with an angry father. The son, Conrad, was a sweet, quiet, indescribably sad young man, a seventh grader, who had been coming to the library regularly all year. He usually sat by himself, sometimes with one other friend. He was never a problem.

One afternoon I was walking a cart of books to the front of the library and I saw Conrad's father open the front door, look briefly around, then squeeze a compressed air horn for several seconds. Then he disappeared. The noise level in the library arced dramatically.

We had already had one unusual run-in with Conrad's dad. One of our friends in the neighborhood reported him because he had parked his car in the library parking lot and was sitting on the hood of his car, gazing at the kids at the junior high school across the street with high-power binoculars. There is no ready explanation that sprang to mind why a person would do such a thing.

Juanita, the head librarian at the time, called the police. The police arrived and spoke to him for about twenty minutes. It seemed a curious thing to them, too. But they told Juanita that it was just Conrad's father trying to get a handle on his son's school. Just Conrad's crazy dad.

Conrad's father was a barrel-chested man in his mid-forties. Perhaps he had been athletic and muscular at one point, but now he was mostly thick. A thick, dark head of hair, double chin, and thin, pale, underdeveloped legs like popsicle sticks. White T-shirt, shorts, and sandals. Conrad will probably look like him in years to come but will be a foot or two taller.

Afterward, he came into the library, wanting to know who had called the police on him, but it turned out he wasn't angry at anyone. He actually thanked us for calling the police, and he said it gave him a good feeling knowing that the library employees were so alert and conscientious. He shook the senior librarian's hands, the assistant librarian's hands, and anyone else's hands he could find, including mine, with a strong and meaty fist. After he left, Juanita was a little leery over the whole thing. It just did not ring true. What father spied on his son's junior high school for an hour at the end of the day? Isn't it a lot easier to simply schedule conferences with your child's teachers? Although he had been friendly and open, there was something about him that spooked us. The hair-on-the-back-of-the-neck thing.

So that was the source of the noise some months later—Conrad's father, in the library, with an air horn. Instead of walking in for a few seconds to find his son and say something like "It's time to go, Conrad," he just opened the front door, let out a blast from an air horn that could be used to signal halftime at a hockey game, and went to wait in his car. Assuming correctly that everyone in the library had heard the noise.

I found Conrad quietly putting his books and papers together, zipping up his backpack, and I asked him to tell his father, please, please, don't use the air horn in the library. It's a pretty loud noise.

I said, "Your dad could come in and look around, it's not that large of a library. Or you could go outside at a certain time each day and wait. We could page you on our public address system. Anything. So tell your dad, okay? No big deal."

Conrad finished putting his books away, smiled, and said, "Okay."

A short discussion, nonadversarial. Well done. I'm the man.

Five minutes later, Conrad's father came into the library. His eyes were glazed red and his hands were trembling. He wanted to know who had humiliated him in front of his son by telling him what he can or can't do. I was behind the counter, and I think, how bad can this get? I told him, well, thanks for coming in, Conrad is a nice kid, but the air horn is awfully loud for the . . .

He pointed a finger at me. "You and I have a problem, son. No one disrespects me like that. In front of my boy. What the hell were you thinking?"

Like a genie summoned by trouble in the library, Juanita was there in the twinkling of an eye, and she introduced herself to Conrad's father, asking him, please, can we take this into my office and talk this all out? She was concerned and obsequious. She took him by the arm and looked at me briefly with wild eyes.

Once we were all in Juanita's office, Conrad's father careened from red-hot anger to great sadness. He said that I was clearly wrong, clearly rude, and should be severely disciplined, even, you know, fired. Conrad was his only son. He was trying to do the right thing here, but when people get in front of him to block him . . . his voice cracked. And out of nowhere he began to talk about his tour of duty in Vietnam, the heat and the stickiness and the overwhelming green humidity of the place, the people in charge who had no idea what they were doing, his friends—brothers—who lost their lives there . . .

Juanita was wearing an expression like she was listening to her best friend talk about the new puppy that ran out the front door and got hit by the SUV. But I know Juanita well enough to know that she was thinking, Where's the closest exit? Is he armed? Is he going to go off again? Can I get him out of here? How? Is he going to leave here and attack someone on the way out? Is anyone on the phone to the authorities? Will I have to make a statement to the media? Did I bring my touch-up case with the really nice blush powder?

And I was thinking, oh shit oh shit oh shit. I was also thinking that he was almost assuredly *not* armed, so when he decided to attack me I would kick him in the knees or the groin, something like that, and then I would run out into the parking lot, so when the police finally arrive they will see him standing over me and will be able to take a few unobstructed shots before he will have a chance to kill me.

Juanita asked me to leave her office so she could talk to Conrad's father alone. She thought that I was making him tense, so with me out of the room he would calm down. She will vamp him. A half hour later, Conrad's father walked out of her office. He came into the break room where we were all waiting and shook my hand with great ceremony. Juanita escorted him to the front door. Conrad was by now asleep in the car.

When Juanita called me back into her office, her face was slack and drained. "Conrad's dad had a few ideas. One is that I should fire you. He said you needed a hell of a lot more training that you obviously had. I told him I would discipline you. Okay, you've been disciplined. Christ. I need a big glass of white wine. I need several. Tell me about the air horn again. I'm going to have to write up an incident report."

Two weeks later, Conrad's father was noticed again, and this time he was selling Hotwheels and boxed Barbie dolls out of his trunk in the parking lot. He had a ton of them and even that was an odd thing to consider. Occaisionally, he glanced at the front windows of the library. Luckily, the windows were tinted and he didn't see me watching him, so I didn't have to smile and wave and pretend I was glad to see him.

Two months after that, at the end of the school semester, Conrad came in to say goodbye to all of us. He has been forced to transfer schools. His father has had some kind of terrible episode and is now residing at the Veterans' Hospital. Conrad will be staying with some relatives in another state for a while.

He already seemed a little older.

More recently, a girl named Rebecca Kim brought her mother in after we had asked her to leave for bad behavior. Rebecca had been slapping people, shouting across the library, and throwing unabridged dictionaries at people. I explained the rules of the library to Mrs. Kim and said that her daughter was probably a fine person, but that we liked to head off this kind of situation by speaking to the parent. Mrs. Kim looked at me and smiled, then turned back to her daughter to find out what the hell I had just said.

Rebecca said, "My mother doesn't speak any English. I will translate."

For the next two minutes, Rebecca Kim gave her mother her version of why she had been thrown out of the library. Her version did not sound like my version at all, and I do not know Korean. Rebecca's version sounded delightful, and several times both Rebecca and her mom shared a nice chuckle. At the end, Mrs. Kim shook my hand, smiling broadly, shaking her head in agreement, and walked out of the library. Rebecca smiled, too, for her own reasons. It was a total success. The parent conference could have gone much, much worse.

Chapter Ten
The Graduates

EVERY YEAR, THE ELEMENTARY SCHOOL graduates a class to the junior high school, the junior high graduates a class to the high school, and the high school graduates a class to whatever comes after that: college, jobs, a stint with the military, a family. Everyone shuttles forward, and as they move forward they change schools, their parents pick up and move to another country, the folks divorce and they are flung to another part of the city, another part of the world, or they sink beneath the tree line and disappear forever. Actually, they all sink beneath the tree line and disappear, but I guess that is life. They are evolving, jettisoning the past and forging new selves. Their old self was a mistake, a misstep, and they cannot go back or they face the embarrassing pain of how they started out.

Everyone on the library staff misses them when they go. We have our favorites. We know that they will never return. Perhaps if they do come back to the library some day with their children, they will look around for a moment, a little embarrassed, and wonder where we are. By that time we, too, will be gone, beneath the tree line. The structure of the building will be the same, the books will be similar, and the carpeting will be of a similar industrial weave and color, but the people they came to recognize will be gone. After a few moments, they will ask someone at the reference desk about us, and these people will shake their heads, for they will have never heard of us either.

About the second or third year I worked in the library, there was Farhad, a young boy of Middle Eastern descent who wore pin-stripe shirts, slacks with built-in belts, and expensive watches. Farhad was only in the seventh grade, and he said he was afraid to tell his parents that he did not want to follow his father into the family busi-ness — some importing, exporting thing — he wanted to be a comedi-an! Farhad was an excellent student, even though he refused to take the educational process seriously. He was always relaxed and sharply dressed, and it was no wonder his father wanted him to take over the business. But Farhad was always looking for the humor in situations and circumstances, not the profit incentive.

His sister was three years older than he, a serious, more somber student, and Farhad hoped to hell his parents would not move the whole family to wherever his sister enrolled in college. But that had always been the plan, and he discovered they were all going to move to Orange County after his sister was accepted at the University of California, Irvine. He told Terri all about his discontent. Do you know all the garage doors in Orange County are painted the same color? Do you know you can't put up a basketball hoop unless you get written authorization? Do you know the ethnic restaurants down there are all crummy? No good Persian food at all!

Farhad's parents let him come visit the library a few weeks after graduation. At home, they were already in cardboard boxes, prepar-ing for the move. Farhad was starting a stamp collection of American plate blocks, and Terri showed him the *Scott's Catalog* that showed all the prices and variations with color pictures of each stamp since the beginning of the country.

He laughed and said he would never have to return it, because we didn't know where he was moving to, and — suckers! — we'd never be able to track him down. He checked the book out, moved, and be-fore it drifted into overdue territory the book was returned in the mail. Inside the front cover was a brief note that read: *I bet you never thought you'd see this book again! Haha. You guys crack me up!*

That Farhad.

There was no Farhad the following fall, and no one else even came close. A lot of the previous year's regulars had moved on and were gone, and when the school year started in September the new crop of students seemed surlier, more nervous and out of control, as if the library was just a place to get in out of the rain or the sun and use the restrooms, and if we didn't like their behavior, fine, they'd leave, muttering and rolling their eyes, flipping us off and laughing as they walked out the door, seized by a recently acquired bravado.

Kevin was one of our first problems to blossom that year. Kevin was a tall, gangly tenth grader. He should have outgrown his goofiness, but he didn't. He made a variety of unusual noises that were detected throughout the library: low guttural coughs, insanely high-pitched squeaks, and lots in between. He made a dripping-water sound that no one else could imitate. One day as I was escorting him to the front door, I asked him why he didn't just go home.

"Mom doesn't get there until about six-thirty," he said.

"Don't you have a key?"

"Hah. Right. No. My stepfather says if I want a key, I should get my own place. Sometimes I get there and his car is out front, he's inside, and he won't even answer the door. He's a jerk pretty much."

Damn this stupid kid, I thought. He is no longer two-dimensional.

Over the next several months Kevin starts talking to me about his life, and I find out that he is a pariah, an outcast. He is Japanese-American, a mix, and he looks it. His father is dead. The stepfather is Japanese. Kevin's stepfather thinks he is a blemish to the family and talks around the house about the day he will be old enough to move out and make his own way in the world.

Kevin looks to his mother for support. His mother looks to the ground. With Kevin's father dead, she does not see a multitude of options. She tells Kevin that, really, his stepfather is a good man . . . and Kevin immediately stops listening. Yeah. Right. He's a peach. Really, Mom.

During the rest of that year, Kevin is a fixture in the library. Juan-ita decides that a good education is Kevin's ticket out. Good grades. Maybe a scholarship. It seems like a long shot, but Juanita sells him on the idea and he says he'll give it a try. He reads, does his homework, flips through magazines, and wiles away the time until he is allowed to go home.

He brings in his next report card. A few C's, a few B's, an A. He is not altogether unimpressed with himself but says that ultimately it will make no difference. His stepfather will say, Why isn't the C a B? Why isn't the B an A? Why aren't they all A's? Perhaps he doesn't even bother to show his report card at home. What's the point? His stepfa-ther will start talking shit, Kevin will eventually give a wise-ass answer that will bubble up out of his mouth before he can stop himself, and his stepfather will give him a smack on the side of his head. Maybe a couple of smacks. He is trying to provoke Kevin into betting into a large pot with bad cards, even Kevin knows that.

Next fall, Kevin is in the eleventh grade, and soon starts asking what our opinion is on him quitting school. We tell him it is a bad idea. We don't have a good alternative, but quitting is bad. His stepfa-ther will undoubtedly throw him out of the house if he drops out, and Kevin has no money, no skills, no place to go, no job.

By Christmas there is a big blowup at home and Kevin moves into a small guesthouse at the back of his grandmother's home. She says she will not charge him rent as long as he stays in school. So he stays in school and takes on two part-time jobs, one of them at a sub shop. Every night, he mops the floors, cleans the meat-slicing ma-chines, and, if the manager isn't there, takes three or four subs home. He makes one especially for his grandmother, without the hot pep-pers. As soon as the manager leaves every evening, Kevin brings out a tip jar that he hides in the cooler, and by the end of the shift he has an-other ten or twelve bucks in his pocket. He saves up his paychecks and buys a sexy used car with a bad muffler that just growls with unbridled power. At school, he gets into the drum line and finds a passion for it. This passion translates to friends, and a few teachers who will back him up when he gets in trouble, which he does often. In the library, he brings in tickets to drum line competitions and leaves them on the reference desk. Says he hopes he will see us there. After he leaves, Juanita picks up the tickets and asks, "What's a drum line competition?" She gives the tickets to Terri, who quietly puts them back on the desk, where they are available to anyone but go unused.

By the twelfth grade Kevin has matured. He takes books out of the library on cooking and invites his younger brother over to his guesthouse for supper. The younger brother wants to flee the stepfather's house too, but Kevin tells him there is not enough room in the small guesthouse for two people. Kevin counsels him, tells him to be patient, stay in the house with his stepfather until he is a little older. Tell Mom he will move out, too, unless he gets a little fucking support. That is not what the brother wants to hear, but it's the truth. He'll have to wait.

Kevin asks out one of the high school volunteers at the library. She is also Japanese-American, petite, shy, and pretty. Part of her would like to go out with him, it seems, but she can't. She's startled that Kevin would even ask her. They have hardly spoken to each other. She has led a sheltered life so far, and Kevin seems exotic and adventuresome. She confides this to Terri, who is more of a neutral sounding board than the girl's own parents or friends. She and Kevin go to the movies on the sly, once. Kevin is looking for something—for sex, sure—but for something else, too. He wants to offer himself to her, but there doesn't seem to be much to offer. The volunteer goes to Terri for help and Terri tells her not to do something if she's uncomfortable doing it. The volunteer tells Kevin she cannot go out with him a second time. So there is no prom. No one from his family goes to his graduation. In the library, we get a card together and put $40 in it. What is $40 to Kevin? Nothing. A kind thought. One trip to the gas station.

After graduation Kevin starts community college for two quarters, then just stops going. It's not what he had hoped for. He thought it would be something of an investment, but it turned out to be a total waste. The thirteenth grade. He wants nothing to do with the college, the professors, the students, or the classes. He sees himself growing older, living in his grandmother's guesthouse, and it is not how he wants to see himself. One day in late fall he comes in and asks if anyone would like to take him out and get him drunk. There is a reason. He has enlisted in the military, and the clock is now ticking on his few remaining days.

We do not take him out and get him drunk. The city frowns on taking underage patrons into bars for strong drink. Instead, we congratulate him and buy him a cake, which we present to him in the abysmal back room of the library. He says he is going to be stationed off the coast of Japan, and the navy has promised to teach him some kind of transferable skill. Maybe electronics. In four years, when he gets out, who knows, maybe he'll be making more money than any of us. We say we hope it is so. He is proud to even think such a thing.

He comes in again, trying to sell us his car. If he gets no takers, he might leave it at his grandmother's house and leave the keys with his little brother. Kind of a going-away present. What he really came in for, though, he says—would anyone like his address, maybe write to him while he is out of the country? Let him know what was going on at the library?

Sure, we say.

When he gets his official address, he says, he'll bring it into the library so we can post it on the bulletin board. Maybe the volunteer who had gone with him to the movies would write to him, too. Yeah. That would be cool. Thanks, he says, looking over his shoulder as he walks out the door, several feet taller than he was only a few years before.

Chapter Eleven
Overdue Fines and Fees

THE LIBRARY WAS NOT SET UP as a money-making institution, and many library administrators have made that fact their moral standard. Actually, most librarians don't understand the "money" thing or the "profit" thing at all. The same librarians will wince and their faces will cloud over when the concepts are explained to them. They are librarians, after all, not shopkeepers. Trying to get a handle on fines and fees and charges is somehow the violation of a sacred trust.

The library has a series of built-in steps in the area of overdue books. On the first overdue day, the computer begins to keep a tally of the fines. After ten days, an automated system calls the patron and tells them in an ominous, unearthly, we-mean-you-no-harm computer voice that library materials are late. After two and a half weeks, the individual library prints out delinquent forms and they are mailed to the patron's address, hinting at some kind of legal action without coming out and saying it. After a month, a real library employee will call the house and make the same vague threat. But it is all bluster. There is no collection agency. No next step. And every five to eight years a new software program is installed to keep up with the demands of the library, and the old delinquency charges, up into the thousands of dollars, are lost forever. But what do we care—we're librarians!

Librarians have less of a sense of camaraderie and goodwill when it comes to damaged, ravaged, and mutilated books. A patron falls asleep in the bathtub and the latest LaVyrle Spencer romance sinks beneath the scented waters. A toddler grabs a crayon and decorates mommy's parenting book while she is taking a nap. A teenager seemingly old enough to know better cuts the color pictures out of a book on George Washington to use in a ten-page report of the first president. A book-on-CD is left on the plane. A pet rat chews the cover off a best seller. A Céline Dion recording is left in the car on a hot afternoon and morphs into something else entirely.

Mrs. Belcher came into the library one Monday morning with a car repair book that was dripping motor oil and was indignant when she heard that we expected her to pay for it. This was the goddamn public library. The free, goddamn public library. What part didn't we get? She was amazed that we expected her to pay for something that was so clearly and obviously an accident.

When that didn't work, she took a different course. According to the library computer, forty other people had checked out the same book over the years. Well, then, it was like taking a bad set of tires back to the store you bought them from. They gauge the amount of tread left in the tire and prorate the true value. The price of the book, long ago when it was new, was $39.95. Forty other people had checked it out. She pursed her lips and did some internal calculations and said she would agree to pay $1/41$ of the book—less than a buck. And to show you where the library's at, we said okay. Soak a book in motor oil, agree to pay back three percent of the book because it's been used and was not in pristine condition in the first place, and there's a good chance the library will be willing to go along with it.

Another fee charged by the library is for requests. A new book comes out by John Grisham—as it seems to do every six weeks or so—and it's so popular that on the day it is returned, someone else will check it back out again. If you decide to wait until the book actually hits the shelves it may take several months. So a request will automatically trap the book and lock it up for a certain patron. For this, the library charges 75 cents—just a little less than the cost of a lottery ticket, where your chance of winning is one in fourteen million. Or one in forty-five million, depending on what state you live in and what "game" you're playing. Yet I have seen patrons debate this charge. Seventy-five cents? What? You're trying to charge me 75 cents for a book you already own? A public library? Charge? You? Me?

One evening, I am sitting at the reference desk when a very young girl and her father are frantically, desperately trying to find blueprints to one of the California missions—*any* of the California missions— because she is studying Father Serra and the missions in school, and if she builds a mission, she will absolutely get a good grade. This is one of the really easy questions. The kids do mission projects every year, and every year they seek out floor plans for the missions. The library has a whole series of books on the California missions, carefully chosen for their pithiness, their sturdy binding, their clarity, the color pictures, and, what else, the floor plans in the back of the book.

Behind them is one of the weekend regulars. He is young, in his late twenties, athletic-looking, and looks like he drives a large truck for a living. Perhaps I believe this because he always wears some sort of baseball hat. But it may be that he wears a baseball hat because his hair is thinning and he has a bald spot he is trying to cover. I don't know.

Long ago, somehow, we bonded. He had come in wearing a Lakers hat, and I said something to the effect that the Lakers were doomed without Shaq—that it had been a stupid trade, that Shaq was more valuable than Kobe, and that Kobe without Shaq, or Coach Jackson, was just going to be a notoriously high scorer on an otherwise ho-hum losing team. Oh, no, he said. Kobe was going to kick the whole team into another gear, and with Butler and Odom and someone else he mentioned, it was a young, hungry team that was only going to get better and better. You'll see.

It felt good to talk like that in the library, guy talk about the NBA and professional athletes instead of the Peloponnesian Wars and heroic couplets and Virginia Woolf and what the green light symbolized in *The Great Gatsby*.

And so we had bonded. It had been a while ago, but there it was. He didn't know my name, I didn't know his, but we knew all we needed to know about each other. He was a regular at the library and I was there to help him.

"I forgot my library card," he said.

This is no big deal in the library. Everyone forgets his library card sooner or later. We have a database. I can look up a patron by driver's license, last name, street address, telephone number, social security number, or several other variables. We charge 50 cents for the service, and pretty much charge at all only because some people would have us do it every time they walked into the library. Fifty cents is a bit of a speed bump. But this guy was a regular, and I, too, am a regular guy, so I said I would waive the 50-cent look-up fee. He said, "I think I might need a whole new card altogether. I haven't been able to find it."

I told him, "If you just want to check some books out today, I'll look your account up. If you think the card is gone for good, I can issue you a new card and that'll cost you five dollars."

"Five dollars," he said. It seemed he was weighing the idea. "I might have some bills, too," he added.

Sure enough, he did. Fourteen dollars in overdue fines. But $14 in overdue fines is not outrageous. Some people always seem to accrue substantial fines and are content to pay them down as they go. Other people are not used to having fines at all, and when you mention the 45 cents worth of fines they have sitting on their account for an overdue picture book, their face will cloud over, all joy will leave them, and they will repeat the name of the book over and over, shaking their head. No, they will finally say, it is clearly impossible. That book was returned on time. They're positive. And you will look at the computer screen that tells you this fine was added to the account more than three months ago. Fourteen weeks. Still, they are sure, it is impossible, they remember bringing the book back on time, because they always bring their books back on time.

If I want, I can palaver. I can say: Give me half and I'll waive the rest. I can say the hell with it, who knows what really happened, I'll waive the whole thing. Or if it is a patron who has done it many, many times because of the exhilaration they get when the library erases a fine, I can say: Well, there it is. Take it or leave it. Sometimes when I am tired I do not like to play this game, and I am tempted to say: Bring the goddamn books back on time and you won't have this problem. But I don't.

I tell the patron in the baseball hat, If you want, pay the $14 in overdue fees and I'll waive the charge for a new library card—which is five dollars. It's at least some kind of a deal. I bring in some revenue for the city, he gets a free library card, and everyone walks away from the transaction feeling they have done well.

But he is suspicious. "What if I just give you five dollars for the new card? How would that be?"

I look at the computer screen again. He has $14 in overdue fines. At the $10 mark the account is blocked. And that is because some patrons would let their fines drift up, up into the hundreds of dollars. "Maybe next time!" they'd laugh evilly each time they left the library with an armful of books. Bwahhahahahahahah! Right! So I tell the guy in the baseball hat that a new library card and a blocked account is a waste of money. You cannot use the card on a blocked account unless the fines are taken back below ten dollars.

He says he will agree to pay four dollars and one cent.

My face begins to cloud over, and all the joy has been sucked out of me. I don't understand people who will pay $10 to sit in a movie theater for two hours but hesitate to pay a 25-cent fine for a book that is overdue one day. I do not understand people who will lustily throw $40,000 at the shiny red automobile of their choice, but well up with tears and become outraged when they are asked to pay $5 for a damaged videotape. Either they are fucked up and their priorities are fucked up or I am fucked up and my priorities are fucked up.

Because I am me, I think it is them.

I think a free library is an outrageous perk. I think being able to take out fifty books at a time is an astounding luxury, especially if you've priced hardbound books anytime since the Clinton administration. Go into a public library, fill out the application, and here you go, we'll loan you $1,000 worth of materials. Collateral? Nah—just take them. You're good for it. We'd do it for anybody.

And we would.

So I tell the patron, sure, if that's how he wants to do it, just give me four dollars and one cent to knock him out of the blocked category, give me five bucks for a new card, and all will be well. It doesn't seem like that much of a deal, and he will still have $9.99 in existing fines. This means if he accrues one more penny in additional fines he's blocked again. But fine.

Yes, he says. That's how he wants to do it.

I look around the library. It is midafternoon on a Saturday in late spring. It is raining slightly. The plants inside the library are uniformly stressed, hard, dry, wanting to die. Well, I tried.

He interrupts my train of thought as I am about to key in a new library card for him.

"What are you doing?" he asks.

"I'm giving you a new library card," I answer. "What this will do, it knocks the old one completely out of the system, so if someone else were to find it on the street and come in and try to use it, it wouldn't . . ."

"No," he says. "That's not what I mean. Where did you get that particular number?"

He is pointing to a bar code that I have attached to a blank library card. I have thousands and thousands of them. Throughout the city, there are thousands and thousands more.

"It's the next one in line," I say. I have no idea what he's talking about.

"I want another number," he says.

I am speechless, but now the clouds in my face are parting and I am getting a little pissed.

"This is the number that gets to be used," I tell him. I am tired of the transaction, tired of the patron. Fuck the Lakers. I will start rooting for the Spurs. It occurs to me that he is perhaps mentally ill. Or he is just screwing with me for his own reasons.

"No. Really. I don't want that number," he says.

I look at the number on the library card, and it does not speak to me the way it has spoken to him. I shrug my shoulders. Lunatic.

"Look," he says, "I'll make you a deal. Give me another library card number and I'll pay the fourteen bucks, all of it, and I'll give you five bucks for the card. Nineteen dollars. Now."

He produces a twenty.

I take another bar code, stick it to another blank library card, and show him the new number. He takes the card in his hand and smiles.

"This one's much better."

I put the information into the computer and do what is required. As for his reasons, I cannot even guess. But I am taking in $19, and that seems good enough for now. Then I give him the card. He gives me the $20 and shakes my hand. He is now one happy guy. He tells me: "You know about that other number, right?"

I don't.

"Mark of the beast," he says. "The Bible. Six six six. Get it?"

I look again at the number. It is a long number, fourteen digits, and around the middle there is a sequence containing "662." Not "666." I look at him.

I think he is a little embarrassed. "Just sixes by themselves are unlucky. Even one. Two of them together, whoa."

I am compelled to play along. He is, after all, a regular and we once bonded long ago talking about the Lakers. "Lucky numbers, unlucky numbers, I get it."

"Sure," he says, comfortable again. "Six six six is the worst, but even one six . . ." He shakes his head. "No good."

"You're not into sixes," I say, stating the obvious.

He shakes his head in deep agreement and leaves the library a happy man, not wretched and accursed like he almost was a few minutes ago for having a six in his library card. And I have completed a successful library transaction, satisfied a customer, and taken in $19 in fines, which the city will use in an enlightened, judicious manner.

Hail Satan!

Chapter Twelve
Wild Animals in the Library

THE BRANCH LIBRARIES GET the most curious junk mail—perhaps the most curious junk mail on the planet. The reason we get it is obvious—we are happy to receive the information. It's part of what we do.

The Monday mail delivery comes in—the nice, beleaguered mail lady smiles and puts it in our hands like she is Bert Parks, the mail is a dozen long-stemmed red roses, and we are the luckiest girl in the pageant. Then she takes the restroom key from the reference desk and disappears for fifteen minutes, like she does every day.

Monday's mail delivery is excess at its finest. There are catalogs, subscription notices, flyers from local restaurants, letters from angry patrons, and regular magazines all bundled together. *Men's Fitness* magazine is on top, and receiving it in the daily mail may be the last time it is touched by human hands. No one in my branch has washboard abs or cares what is required to get them. The fifty-five-year-old men at my branch are indifferent to their glutes, their pecs, their quads, or any other muscle group you could identify. Juanita ordered the subscription several years ago, shortly before she was promoted, and everyone figured she had checked the wrong box in a hurry to meet her golden destiny.

This Monday, there is also a *Sunset Magazine*, a *National Geographic*, a skateboarder magazine that will surely disappear in days, and an *Elderhostel*. *Elderhostel* is an oversize, quarterly publication that gives seniors the inside dope on how to spend their remaining time on earth. The demographics are dead on, but the economics are off.

The elderly at my branch are trying to avoid the 25-cent daily late fee on the Agatha Christie novel they've forgotten to return. They've lived in the same house and read the same newspaper for forty years and are pleasantly surprised when someone explains that the house they bought for $40,000 in 1950 is now worth upwards of six to seven hundred thousand dollars, but it is not the same thing as being well off. They have nowhere they want to move, no place to go, so the housing price is a bit of a joke. All it does is raise their property taxes. They are still living on fixed incomes, still living modestly, still cutting coupons, still on the lookout for the early-bird specials at chain restaurants. They come to the library trying to find an 800 number so they can complain about the gaps in their health insurance. They are not up to pricing a ten-day stay at a volcanic hot springs somewhere in Greenland. They are just trying to fall apart gracefully.

There is also a single youth magazine with pictures of Gwen Stefani, Justin Timberlake, and Jessica Simpson on the cover. In a few weeks, this magazine will be ready to be thrown out. There will be pages pulled out, questionnaires dutifully penned in and answered, articles and pictures scissored out, and the cover itself will be vile— Jessica will have several teeth blackened out, her eyes will be crossed, and stylized, primitive cocks will be drawn in, pointing to the vandal's favorite stars.

In any case, once the paid subscriptions have been winnowed out, the rest is an odd lot. There is a notice from a local hydrangea society—Don't forget the membership meeting on the fourteenth! There is a plea from a local animal rights group asking that we all neuter our pets and there are accompanying pictures of emaciated, abused animals in case we fail to make the connection. There is a full-color brochure from the local light opera association, reminding us to renew our subscriptions for what will almost assuredly be the best damn year of light opera in the South Bay ever.

There is a notice from a group called something like Who's Who in Raised Bed Gardening. Would we like to be included in next year's listing? Anyone? As long as they've got our attention, would we like to buy a copy? The answer—although we never actually take the time to answer them—is always no. We don't want any part of it. We know it's all a scam, a thing to see your name in print. For Christ's sake, we're not going to *buy* one. But no one on staff is compelled to let them know this, so we will get the same offer next year, too.

The most curious thing in the daily junk mail, and this is saying a lot, is the advertisements by local, mostly amateur performers who saturate the libraries with their peppy proposals and postcards. Jugglers. Magicians. Puppeteers. Whatever you call people who work marionettes. Improvisational troupes. People who can play unusual and easily portable musical instruments.

The idea is that, for a modest fee, they will pack the library with happy children. They'll perform their show, the kids will have a good time, and before they leave a children's librarian will uncoil before them and strike before they hit the front door. Before their unsuspecting parents know what has happened, they will all have library cards and we will be able to include them in our monthly statistics.

To a small child, a live performance is a heady experience, a scaled-down Woodstock without the music and the drugs. You are sitting several feet away from Chauncey, the Singing Dragon, and he is telling you interesting tales about recycling and saving the planet. Jimmy the Puppet Guy is pulling kids up on stage beside him to help with a skit about oral hygiene or obesity. It is too fun. These are little kids—they don't know any better. They think they're having a good time.

Terri, who has been the children's librarian for a while now, gathers up all the promotional postcards and collects them in a three-ring binder labeled "Performance Artists." She has a variety of these binders, grouping information intelligently on different topics. Other librarians are ashamed of their organizational skills when they see Terri's binders. They don't realize that Terri has an unfair advantage—she has obsessive compulsive disorder. She feels as if she is staving off some personal calamity by putting things in order. Given that she works at the library, she is probably correct. It is a happy coincidence that her career choice is made stronger by an identifiable psychological disorder. Life is funny.

In the "Performance Artists" binder, each postcard is taped to its own page. The pages are sequenced alphabetically, and noted on each sheet is the price of the performance, group discounts (if any), comments by other librarians who have used the performer, and the approximate age range of kids who might be interested in such a thing.

One of the first programs Terri brought to the library was a memorable one. Through a public affairs branch of the police department, she hired an absolute stud of a policeman and his drug-sniffing dog. It was called something like "Patrolman Mike and his Pal Raffles Talk About Making Good Life Choices." Raffles, a well-muscled German shepherd, weighed about 80 pounds.

Patrolman Mike was a trained public speaker whose voice was so round and clear and modulated that he didn't need a microphone. He weighed about 190. When he spoke, wherever you were standing, you understood him. He had a thick head of hair, an easy demeanor, and great teeth. As did Raffles. Twenty kids at a time could stroke and scratch and pull at the dog, and he wouldn't growl or snap at any of them. The dog was utterly calm.

What did excite Raffles was drugs—drugs in suitcases, drugs in hubcaps, wherever someone thought they could be hidden. It didn't matter. In concentrations as low as four or five parts per million, Raffles made the connection. And, whenever Raffles made the connection, Patrolman Mike rewarded him with a big hug and a doggy treat, then told him to "Sit!" and "Stay!" while he called in the bust and began filling out the paperwork.

The branch kids loved the performance. Patrolman Mike said, "We all know that drugs are a bad choice, right, kids?" The kids needed no prompting, and screamed out the correct answer. Raffles looked unconcerned. Patrolman Mike continued, "We all know that reading a good book is a much better high than injecting crank underneath our tongues, right, kids?" Then he winked at Terri, who caught the wink and buckled slightly. Good-looking policemen are near the top of one of Terri's many lists, as is Johnny Depp, firemen, and pirates in general. Terri's husband, Curtis, is at the absolute top of the list, so the rest of it is hypothetical.

"Okay," Patrolman Mike said. "We're going to play a game, if that's all right with Miss Terri?"

Terri giggled and shook her head. "Of course," she answered in a husky voice, totally inappropriate to the library.

The policeman held up a sock and explained that it was a very special sock. It had been imbued with the essence of crack cocaine and marijuana. A sachet, if you will. And we're going to hide the sock somewhere in the library. Anywhere! And Raffles here is going to go find it. Aren't you, Raffles? He waved the sock briefly in front of the dog and the dog sprang to attention, ready for the game.

"Okay, who wants to hide the sock?" Patrolman Mike asked, and forty to fifty small hands flew into the air. Patrolman Mike picked a young Indian boy who immediately went back to his seat and stuffed the sock inside his shirt, chuckling like the cleverest of madmen. But Raffles had been watching the whole thing. His eyes were wide, his muscles coiled, ready to fly across the small space, and Patrolman Mike knew immediately that *this* wasn't going to end well. So another, slightly older boy was chosen, and this boy ran off laughing into the large-print biographies to do his job.

After another three or four minutes of shtick, Patrolman Mike unclipped Raffles from his leash, who was now lunging forward and moaning in anticipation of the game. Patrolman Mike said, "Seek, Raffles! Seek!" The dog flew in the direction of the large-print biographies, and the crowd screamed in delight. But instead of running straight into the large-print biographies, Raffles stopped at the end of the first aisle, took a sniff, quivered, and ran like a crazed beast into the automotive section where he ripped the purse out of the hands of a surprised twenty-two-year-old girl and ran it back to Patrolman Mike.

The girl had been wandering around looking for a repair manual for her boyfriend's 1988 Chevy Impala. She had no idea there was a dog in the library that was a much better judge of weed than she was. Patrolman Mike told Raffles "Release! Sit! Stay!" and gave the dog a special doggy treat. Then he returned the purse to the speechless young woman, telling her maybe she should go sit outside in front of the library for, oh, say fifteen or twenty minutes. Until the show was over. This was a gig, not a bust. He didn't even open up the purse. The girl understood. She went and sat outside the library, and within five minutes she got into her car and drove away. She really, really understood.

Another show Terri arranged was called "Kathy's Animal Friends," out of San Bernardino County. On the postcard there was a picture of Kathy, smiling, quite the charmer, along with a cockatoo on her shoulder, a millipede wrapped around her wrist, some sort of stuporous lizard clinging to her shirt, and a large, nightmarish beetle scuttling around in her lap. It was a hell of a photograph. The caliber of the animals was a little tame but her demeanor was very appealing. She seemed calm and at peace with the animals. She looked like she'd be good with kids. Terri had a long conversation with her on the phone and booked her on instinct alone.

"She lives on a big piece of land out in the desert, all by herself," Terri explained. "I guess she *had* a boyfriend who helped out for a while, but she said he went off on some archaeological dig in South America about five months ago and never came back. She still gets letters from him, but they're through as a couple. Anyway, she has something like a compound and takes in all kinds of animals—a lot of wild animals that rich people get and then decide they can't take care of. You know? She seems really nice. I'm going to see if the Friends of the Library can chip in a few hundred dollars on this one."

On the day of the performance, Kathy brought in the aforementioned cockatoo and millipede, along with a kinkajou, a marmoset, a ferret, and a nice selection of the nightmarish bugs that would have been winners all by themselves. Before showing them to the kids, Kathy gave an introduction, talked about each creature, and then brought them out with a flourish, to collective gasps and awe. Some of the animals got to be petted and handled, while others were shy, she said, and didn't like to be touched. A few of the kids dared to hold the millipede. The marmoset, which looked like a miniature cheetah only a little larger than a house cat, was paraded around a bit, but it began to act skittish and nervous so Kathy tucked it back in a cage draped with a blanket.

After the performance, while Terri and a few of the pages were putting the juvenile section of the library back together again, Terri noticed an itching sensation in her legs that became increasingly unpleasant. Her arms began to itch and, at the same time, her face flushed and her eyes began to water. By eleven that night her skin was on fire, her limbs were swollen, and both she and her husband Curtis assumed she had somehow been bitten by a tick or a mite or some kind of wild animal–related parasite.

Even later that night, Curtis drove her to the emergency room where they began to stabilize whatever the hell was wrong with her. In the middle of the needles and IV drips and tongue swabs, it occurred to Terri that whatever was happening to her could be happening to the children who had been at the show, earlier in the day. She asked Curtis to check the waiting area of the emergency room and was only partially reassured when Curtis reported there were no swollen, itchy, purple-skinned children elsewhere in the building.

Early the next morning, she called library administration from her bed to let them know what had happened, and to suggest, you know, maybe closing the library until someone figured out what was going on. Terri felt worse than she already did, lying there, thinking that just as this "thing" had jumped onto her, it could have also jumped onto one of the happy little kids she remembered from the day before.

In the next twenty four hours an allergist was brought in to see if he could shed some light on the situation. He, too, would have been a successful library program all by himself. He drew a large grid on her back with a felt-tip pen and, from left to right, top to bottom, tested her for a different allergy in each square. In the end, he said that it was his opinion that she was allergic to the marmoset and had somehow inhaled animal dander—although he really didn't see how that was possible un- less she had already been exposed to marmosets in the past. That is how allergies work. You have to have had a previous exposure. He checked her out for chocolate, goose feathers, perfume, bee venom, semen, dust mites, bamboo, cotton, grass, latex, cheese, milk, flour, peanuts, and a great many other things, but there was no square in his grid for marmo- set. Yet nothing else made sense. Millipedes? Nah. Lizards? Not even if it had bitten her in the face. No, the marmoset was the most likely candidate. He made a face like—well, what are you going to do?—and shrugged his shoulders. He had never even heard of marmosets before, and Terri didn't have a picture to show him.

The allergist notified workman's compensation, workman's compensation notified library administration, and four days later the library sprang into action and had Mr. Weams and his janitorial crew shampoo the entire floor of the library and wipe down every surface in the library with a minty disinfectant.

When Mr. Weams saw me in the library that morning, he beck- oned me to him as he hunched over the rug shampoo machine. Admin- istration had given him only the most bare bones of stories, and he was covered in sweat and clearly not enjoying himself.

"So, what's going on?" he asked. "How's that Terri girl? I'm hear- ing all kinds of different stories. Poor thing. She still in the hospital?"

I told him what I knew. She had been discharged by the hospital, she was out of danger, and the allergist warned her not to return to work until the swelling had gone completely and the area the animals had been in had been completely scrubbed down.

Mr. Weams wiped his face with a bandanna and shook his head. "That's good, that's good. She got to take care of herself. City don't give a damn."

Mr. Weams was in no mood to continue working.

"Ain't that always the way? We get an emergency call out to come to the branch library and shampoo the rugs—*something* might be in the rugs to send a person to the hospital. See what I'm getting at? Like, who the hell are *we*?"

Oh, I knew exactly what he was getting at. He was just a janitor, an expendable, black janitor.

Mr. Weams nodded. "You got that right. Expendable, as always. 'Oh, look—there's some depleted uranium. Go get yourself a plastic bag and some rubber gloves and clean it up.' Someone winds up going to the hospital, they'll be all 'Oh, my gracious! We had no idea!'" He held a meaty fist to his bosom like a startled southern belle. Mr. Weams is a trip.

Mr. Weams is so close to retirement that it makes absolute sense to him that the city deliberately puts him in harm's way. His anger is like a big multivitamin for his immune system. "Lordy, lordy, lordy," he says in resignation, wiping away some more sweat with a forearm. "White people. Goddamn crazy white people. Gonna kill us all." He is leaning on the rug shampoo machine that will hopefully get rid of the marmoset dander that may or may not be the cause of Terri's current condition.

The week Terri returns, she writes a long letter to the editor for *Library Journal*, a monthly magazine written for librarians and interesting to no one else. She isn't sure what the answer is to her cautionary tale, but it seems the library is letting itself open to risk. How can we better police ourselves? How can we protect our children? What can we do differently in the future? Is something like this even preventable?

Her letter does affect one small change. A few months later, we have gotten ourselves on another mailing list and begin receiving a complimentary copy of *Library Journal* at the branch. Addressed to Terri, it comes in the mail along with *Popular Science, Rolling Stone, Martha Stewart Living, Baby Bug, Cook's Illustrated,* and the *Kelley Blue Book* guide for used cars.

Chapter Thirteen
The Friends of the Library

THE FRIENDS THAT HELPED Terri pay for the wild animal show that almost killed her is a nonprofit group dedicated to supporting the library in its many endeavors. Most of the time they are simply referred to as the "Friends." You might, for example, hear the sentence, "There's not enough money in the city budget to buy a new shelving unit for our DVDs, but the Friends might be persuaded to buy us one." You hear a sentence like that and your mind might grind to a stop. Not enough money in the city budget, but the friends will take care of it? You think, who the hell are these friends? Who are these pro-library, free-spending, deep-pocketed friends? Are they my friends, too?

After a few years, the linguistic construction becomes clear. Whenever people chat about the Friends of the library, it is a capitalized word. It is a proper noun. A group. And when you hear the word in a sentence, it is not only capitalized, there are quotation marks around it. They're not your friends. They're the "Friends." More specifically, the "Friends of the Library." The Friends raise money throughout the year and spend it all on the library. They buy expensive security systems, Internet access, and a lot of other things nobody thought it would cost that much to buy ahead of time. They are all retired. They are men and women in their sixties, all retired. It is some kind of cool job.

At every branch, book donations are gratefully accepted. The donations are bundled together, tied together with string or tucked into plastic tubs or orange crates, and sent along to the main branch. There, the Friends have a holding area in the basement, where they sort through the donations. Several times a year, the books are dollied upstairs by the beefier library pages into a large meeting room and then offered for resale to the general public. The sale of this material generates big bucks.

What gets donated?

Everything. Hardbound books signed by Dean Koontz, Art Buchwald, Lawrence Welk, and Ernest Hemingway. Art books that weigh forty pounds. Comic books. *National Geographic* magazines that date back to the early 1920s. *Reader's Digest* condensed best sellers. Current best sellers. Mechanical diagrams. Schematics. Textbooks. Travel books for countries no longer found on the map. Full-color manuals for nursing students on diseases of the foot, infections of the brain, and trauma to the eye. Kids' books that play tinny electrical songs when you open them. Books on how to field-dress quail and deer. Books on how to live nicely after a nuclear holocaust. Books on how to make a redwood deck. The rules of chess. If you are a member of the Friends of the Library and see all this stuff, it is like running your hands through pirate treasure. The mundane and the exotic in vast piles.

One of the more exciting donations to our library in recent history was deposited in our outside bookdrop long after the library was closed. The next morning, it filled the bookdrop to the brim. All of the titles were remarkably similar: *Storage and Usage of Plastic Explosives*, *A Common Sense Guide to Piano Wire and the Garrotte*, *Changing Your Appearance Without Surgery*, *Fifty Guaranteed Death Blows*, and *The Many Forms of Anthrax*. Juanita went through the pile with a clenched jaw and wondered if we should send the books to the Friends or have them dusted for prints by the FBI.

Terri put an unreasonably optimistic spin on the donation. "A real terrorist wouldn't bother donating this kind of thing to the public library. They'd just throw it away. You think they want to be known a hundred years from now for their recycling efforts? It was probably some old guy who's been reading a few too many Tom Clancy and James Bond novels, and his wife finally put her foot down and threatened to divorce him unless he got rid of the stuff."

One of the pages who desperately wanted to believe this was much relieved by the theory. "Yeah. If you were a terrorist and owned these books, would you throw them away in the first place? You'd burn them or something. Or put them in plastic bags and take them to a Dumpster. And if you were a terrorist, would you live around here?" He waved his arms around to indicate "here."

"Now, now," Juanita interrupted, which meant: I don't agree with this line of thinking at all. This would be a lovely place to live if you were a terrorist.

Over the next few days, there were additional donations of this kind of material to the bookdrop. Books such as *Everything Is a Weapon* and *Delivering Non-Lethal Pain*. We all tried to convince ourselves of Terri's hypothesis—that some long-suffering housewife had finally laid down the law. The Friends were delighted with this donation. Someone would gobble up this stuff at the next book sale, and it would all be gone by noon.

One of the biggest scores they ever had was a leather-bound physician's reference book, hand-signed by one of the first colonial physicians, dated in the early 1600s. The Friends sold it at a private auction for thousands and thousands of dollars.

At my branch we once received a cardboard box filled with books they used to sell in the theater during the intermission at first-run movies. *The Making of "My Fair Lady," Ben-Hur, The Story of Maria von Trapp*, and *Who Was Spartacus?* We've also received a stamp collection, rare sheet music, and, once, a collection of oil paintings. We weren't sure about the oil paintings. It was local talent, and only barely. Sleeping puppies. Cats watching a rain storm through a pane of glass. A small child blowing on a dandelion. Uniformly repulsive, worthless stuff, but the Friends were glad to have it. They sold the paintings for five to ten dollars apiece. Half of the people who bought them thought they were breathtaking. The other half realized they were odious and planned to paint over them and use the canvases again.

Flip through the books donated and there's another level of wonder: twenty-dollar bills used as bookmarks, seventy-year-old receipts to defunct famous restaurants, church bulletins, doodles on napkins, sketches, and boarding passes to flights that landed in 1971.

As far as I can figure, a person dies, the next of kin grievingly hightails it to the house and immediately wheels out the Sony Trinitron, pries up a few floorboards in a fevered, unsuccessful search for the gold Krugerrands, sells the worthwhile furniture, and eventually jettisons the rest. No one thinks of finding hidden treasure in books. If they're thinking of reselling the house, the piles of books have to go.

No doubt.

To a mover, boxes of books are a more accursed item than a grand piano. They are the most cumbersome things to move, and they take the most time. They're heavy. They are covered in dust. And there's a good chance the books have never been opened, much less read, in a decade. When a bookmark tumbles out of an old book pristine and unwrinkled, it is like a gasp of breath from another century.

The Friends are relegated to the basement of the main branch of the library, a sprawling, hockey rink–sized area that is covered floor-to-ceiling with temporary shelving. What was in a particular area will not be there in two weeks' time. It is all moving, a slow-motion glacier of printed materials. The magazines are segregated, the recent fiction is segregated, everything is discerned and grouped and separated and held, then disgorged to an eager public on the day of the book sale. Fill a shopping bag for ten dollars. Buy a hardbound book for a dollar. Take a chance on an exotic travel guide for $2.50. Why not?

At the end of the day of the book sale, whatever is left over has no excuse. Hundreds of bargain-crazed people have surged through the aisles, touching and considering everything. Parents buy the kids' books, students buy the textbooks, and foreigners buy the foreign books. The curious buy whatever strikes their fancy, and scary eBay entrepreneurs buy whatever they think will sell on the Internet. Often, when they're wrong, they donate the books to the library a second time and receive an official receipt for their taxes.

The leftovers are thrown into a large Dumpster rented specifically for the event. A private contractor gives the city so much per pound for the nonremarkable leavings, and at least it guarantees that the flotsam will move on and be recycled. Even so, every few years a curious taxpayer will peer into a Dumpster late at night and be outraged at the waste. What?! Libraries throwing away printed material? While some wretched homeless person, some unwed mother, some bored prisoner could be reading this!

The situation is a little different at the branch libraries, like mine. There are five different branches scattered throughout the city. They are smaller than the main branch, have fewer staff, and much smaller budgets. The hours are different. The branches cater to specific nearby demographics and have more of a community feel. Some patrons enjoy the main branch for the breadth of its resources, and others prefer the branch libraries for their personal attention and folksiness. For this reason, patrons donate their used books and videos and CDs to a particular library with gusto. After a long weekend, there can be several cardboard boxes piled high next to the front door. And all week long, regularly and unpredictably, patrons will come in with their donations: a small plastic bag of best sellers, a tied bundle of impressive, glossy coffee table books, a shopping bag full of lurid romance novels with long-haired muscular pirates, swooning redheads with huge breasts, and angry unshackled slaves, ready to do something really sexual to the pink-cheeked Civil War cuties in front of the destroyed plantations, symbolic flames already leaping out of the second-story windows.

I am in charge of the sorting and winnowing in the back room, away from the eyes of the public. We will keep the best sellers if we don't already have them and it looks like they will circulate. We will keep large chunks of the romance novels—we put them in bins by the side windows and they circulate like crazy. Women come in and take up to a hundred at a time. Sometimes they keep them forever; sometimes they bring them back and take another hundred. We don't care. There are always too many of them.

The older, hardbound books we tie up in ten-pound bundles and send them along to the Friends with the oversized $60 coffee table books, the textbooks, the histories, the glossy Hollywood biographies, and the auto repair manuals.

What we don't send, and what they don't want, are books ruined by mold, mildew, and water, books infested with insects, books eaten by rats, books with sections pulled out, books colored in by children, and books just plain ruined and falling apart. Oh, and *National Geographic* magazines and *Reader's Digest* condensed novels, even if they're in really, really good shape. If I hear an insect so large he is scuttling around inside the cardboard box, I pitch the whole box.

We have this large trash container at our branch that is black and plastic and anonymous. Each and every week we fill it with several hundred pounds of books. We top it off with old *Los Angeles Times* newspapers to hide our secret shame. Also, we don't want some Dumpster-diving busybody writing angry editorials to the local newspapers.

The Friends have to sort through the rest and direct the constant stream of printed materials to the right pile for the book sales. Every morning, they put out several book troughs at the main branch with the best of the recent donations—slam-dunk material. Best sellers might go for three dollars, an expensive art book on Picasso might go for six, and a nice, clean children's book might be a buck. Patrons nibble at them all day long, touching and buying, and on some days the troughs will have to be restocked by midafternoon.

Financially, the Friends are doing well. Within the past twelve months, they have purchased a large movie screen for the main library to show outdoor movies in the park, they have approved of several elaborate pieces of furniture for the branches to display audiovisual material, they kick in for pizza and sodas at the monthly teen book group, and they keep the children's librarians stocked with crayons, glue sticks, construction paper, and whatever else is needed to keep small children happy and occupied.

Their largest donations go toward computers—public Internet terminals in every branch, scores of them in the main library, and everything associated with them: color monitors, hard drives, antivirus protection, surge protectors, and a variety of software programs.

It is quite an act of faith for the Friends to do this. Generationally speaking, the Friends are not totally at ease around computers. These are retired people, people old enough to remember World War II. They are familiar with razor blades, reel-to-reel tape recorders, spray antiperspirant, tape recorders, LPs, and the big band sound. Most of the Friends do not Google. But they have faith in the idea of the thing, and so they subsidize the library Internet. The costs are unending. By the time they have outfitted the main and five branches with computers and Internet access, it is just about time to start thinking about pulling it all out and updating the equipment. If they make one large buy and install them one branch at a time, some of the equipment will be close to obsolescence before it gets out of the shipping box.

The Friends are associated with the library but are not part of the library. They do not hold their meetings in the library. You cannot call the library and be connected to an extension for the Friends. Library employees as a rule do not know the names of the Friends. If there is a hierarchy in the Friends, library personnel are ignorant of it.

Within the last six months I was called to the front desk because of another unusual donation. A patron came in and donated what looked like several pages of illuminated script and a half dozen religious etchings. The woman said they had been in her aunt's attic. Her husband had almost thrown them away. He had been throwing away the aunt's junk all day long, and to him this looked like more junk.

We brought the material into the back room, called the main library, got an outside number for the Friends, and that afternoon a specialist from the Friends pulled into the parking lot in an old station wagon, the back of which was filled with bundles of old, hardbound books. The windshield of the station wagon was cracked, the exhaust was rattling out smoke, and the front license plate had been tied on with what looked like blue yarn.

I had never seen him before. He looked at the donation and called another one of the Friends and told him to meet him at his home. Pronto. It looked like the stuff would be worth a few thousand, at least. They would probably run it by an appraiser they knew in West Los Angeles, maybe sell it to an individual who put a lot of that stuff up on eBay.

Before he left, he looked at a few of the bundles tied up and ready to go. He took five of them and threw them into the back of his station wagon, making it rock like a hammock. Something was seriously wrong with the car's shocks. Then he took a peek into the Dumpster, took out a four-year-old Fodor's guide to France, began to thumb through it, said, "Nah!" and threw it back in.

Before he left, a middle-aged woman brought in yet another shopping bag of romance paperbacks. "Ah, hell," he muttered to himself and threw the shopping bag on top of the other bundles, making the station wagon rock like a hammock again.

Chapter Fourteen
Volunteers

MY PARENTS — MY MOTHER, REALLY —constantly tried to instill in me the value of a dollar, but I declined the education. What
did I care if I had money in my pockets? Their arguments were wasted
on me. So my mother cleverly went all reverse psychology on me
and pulled in the opposite direction. Doing a thing for free and not
expecting anything at all in return. This was, I assumed, the reason
she taught Sunday school each week, which was as thankless as a job
could get.

But when I asked about it she shook her head, no. "I'm atoning,"
she replied, daring me to ask the next logical question.

"For what?" I asked. I was so easy in those days.

"You," she said, simultaneously snubbing out and lighting up
another cigarette. "You."

For some reason, I made a Sunday school teacher cry one Sunday when I was a kid. She was an older German lady with blue hair,
and there were four or five of us in her class, all boys, and I thought
we were just amusing her with our antics through the brutal, hour-
long class. But this was not the case. The woman called our house
one Sunday afternoon and unburdened her soul to my mother. My
mother never gave me a blow-by-blow of the whole conversation, but

within the week she had signed up for the now empty position as a sort of penance for having a terrible son.

It took me until college to figure out the wisdom of having money in my pocket, and this had to do with confronting the opposite sex. At Ohio State, witty banter was fine, wearing clean clothes right side out was a step in the right direction, but nothing really went further in establishing that first, tenuous relationship than the ability to spring for a round of Putt-Putt or a movie without counting the change in your pockets. For years my parents tried unsuccessfully to instill in me a healthy respect for the value of a dollar. In the end, a bored young woman in an angora sweater and blue jeans sitting by herself in a college bar called the South Heidelberg accomplished the job in seconds without either of us saying a word.

In college I would do almost anything to get spending money. One of the more memorable jobs I ever had was wearing a fiberglass Mr. Peanut outfit and roaming through malls and supermarket grand openings, doling out airline-serving-sized bags of free peanuts. The costume had obviously been designed and built by people who would never have to wear it. It was impossible to put on by yourself, difficult to see out of, and hard to navigate in. I imagined it was something like an early Soviet spacesuit.

Mr. Peanut wore a tall, zany, black fiberglass top hat, so the get-up was also top-heavy. If I tried to look down and see if my shoes were tied, there was a good chance I'd tip forward and hurl myself into the Pampers display. Which I did. One of the supermarket assistant managers had to rush over and help me right myself. The gesture was not magnanimous on his part. He peered into my manacled peephole and asked if I had been drinking—such was his opinion of college students performing corporate tasks.

At one of my many Mr. Peanut events I ran into one of my buddy's girlfriends. Her name was Debby. She, too, was on the corporate payroll. She was dressed in some executive's fantasy of a German fräulein, complete with lederhosen and a frilly bodice that accentuated her breasts, and she wandered through the same aisles of the supermarket I did, giving out packages of free cigarettes to people who had so far avoided the addiction.

"What a stupid costume," I muttered to her through my peephole. She knew who I was immediately. One of her boyfriend's idiot pals.

"Isn't it hot in there?" she asked with motherly concern. Because she was someone else's girlfriend, she could afford to be kind and solicitous without having me take it the wrong way.

"I'm sweating like a dog in here. The straps holding the costume on straight are cutting into my shoulders. And I can't wipe the sweat out of my eyes unless I go to the back room and take the whole thing off. It's a great gig."

"Poor thing," she said, and for a moment I stared at the corporate fräulein and wondered if she'd dump her boyfriend for a run at a prince like me. But the moment passed. She was commiserating with Mr. Peanut, not me. So I gave her several dozen packages of peanuts and she passed me a carton of cigarettes. We were just two corporate icons passing in the night.

The easiest money I ever made was when I passed myself off as an entertainer for a wealthy Columbus doctor for his once-a-year soiree. The index card at the Student Union jobs board had called for a harpist, but the note had been hanging there for over two weeks. No harpists seemed to be beating a path to his sumptuous oaken door. The dinner party was fast approaching and, in real estate parlance, I smelled a motivated buyer, so I called him.

He sounded so relieved. Did I play the harp? Why, no. But I played the accordion. He thought about it for a moment. Did I know any Irish music? I saw where he was going with this—there were going to be servants, caterers, linen tablecloths, candles on every table, strange and grotesquely festive centerpieces, a large, quiet black man in cook's whites slicing off oh-so-tasty pieces of prime rib, and a red-haired colleen strumming a harp in the corner, playing "The Wild Colonial Boy" in such a way as to break your heart in a million tiny pieces.

Yes, I said. I know a lot of Irish songs. A *lot*. Oh yes. Tons.

So he gave me the address, told me when to show up, and said I'd be taking home forty bucks at the end of the night.

I really didn't know any Irish music. I'm German. I know polkas. I went through my music books back at the dorm and found only a few numbers. "Oh, Danny Boy" was one of them, along with "My Bonny Lies Over the Ocean," which I hoped was Irish and not some goddamn nursery rhyme. I also decided to learn "A Shanty in Old Shanty Town," because I was desperate and because it had a pretty melody. "Shanty" was an Irish term, right? They lived in shanties. Right? Jesus, I hoped so. I really needed the money to impress a waitress at a Greek restaurant whose brothers had already warned me to leave their sister alone.

I showed up at the right time and on the right day—which is one of my strengths—and even wore a tie. Playing the accordion with a tie on is madness. The accordion presses into your tie, the tie squeezes against your larynx and cuts off the blood supply to your brain, and you are constantly on the verge of autoasphyxiation.

I was insidious. I played "Oh, Danny Boy" in a corner of the room—the long version, not the one you hear on the radio—and watched unobtrusively as the nurses and neonatal specialists chatted, laughed, clinked glassware, nibbled hors d'oeuvres, and drank.

And oh, how they drank. Cases of French wine. Glasses of scotch with the kind of ice cubes you could never make at home. The occasional bottle of imported beer. There were three bartenders in attendance, and the reeling medical specialists kept them constantly and furiously busy.

They were drinkers.

At the end of the first hour of the dinner party I had exhausted my meager repertoire of Irish music and had begun to play things like "Love Me Tender" in what I thought would be a romantic, beaten-down-by-the-British, Irish-y way. Little by little, the men abandoned the good French wines and drifted into harder liquors. I, too, drifted, eventually hammering out numbers like "Roll Out the Barrel" and "She's Too Fat for Me." At one point my employer looked at me and smiled, obviously savoring the wisdom of his decision. We were onto show tunes now, and the crowd was singing along to songs like "Matchmaker, Matchmaker" from *Fiddler on the Roof*. The harpist would have retreated to the kitchen by now, or fled in tears.

Around 1:30 a.m. my employer walked me to my car, pressed eighty bucks into my hand, and said, "Christ, you know a whole *boatload* of Irish music." I do not think he was being sarcastic.

I still have the same battered accordion. One of my daughters borrowed the case as a prop for a high school production of *The Music Man*, and now there are letters painted on the side that read "Professor Harold Hill."

Years later, the idea of doing something for nothing finally occurred to me, and I started volunteering my services as an accordion player at a small library adjacent to Bay City. The children's librarian there was an open, optimistic, what's-the-worst-that-can-happen sort of woman, and she urged me to bring in my accordion for one of her regular Tuesday evening storytimes. Her name was Carla and she had zero budget, tsunami-like enthusiasm, and a story hour scheduled for the first Tuesday of every month except December, at 7 p.m. During her stint as a children's librarian, Carla hosted group sings, darned hand puppets, baked cookies, read children's stories using different voices, told folktales by the light of a flickering jack-o'-lantern, played the zither, charmed city officials into donating prizes for her summer reading program, donated her own money to buy supplies, and learned how to fold origami to punch up a few of her stories. The kids adored her. And why not? It was obvious she adored them.

While Carla set up her flannel boards or transitioned to a story using finger puppets, I played the accordion. It felt good to make that much noise in a place that is so traditionally quiet. I've played in bars, living rooms, restaurants, convalescent homes, even twenty-four-hour laundromats, but nothing beats the perverse thrill of playing "Under the Double Eagle" in a place where you're usually glared at for speaking in a normal voice.

The first evening was a pleasant success. Little kids are a very forgiving and charitable audience. If they know they're there to hear stories and have fun, that's what they set their minds to do. The parents were relaxed, too. That is part of the underlying beauty of free programs at the library. At no time does anyone think "What the hell is going on here? I paid ten bucks for this?" No sir. It was all free. At the end of the program, Carla gave away coloring sheets to take home and she raffled off a five-dollar gift card to a local bookstore. The parents congratulated Carla, Carla thanked me, and the next Tuesday evening the same kids were there, plus a few more. That was always Carla's goal: a few more.

At the end of the first performance, one mom was waiting for me with her five-year-old son by Carla's office. She had red hair. He had red hair. She said: "My son wants to ask you a question."

"Shoot," I told her.

Her son was hiding behind his mother's back. I could see his hands, holding on to her hips. He was like a little U-boat captain scanning the Atlantic for solitary freighters.

"I'm shy, too," I told him.

He peeked out behind his mother.

"Go ahead, honey," she told him.

It took him a few seconds to get his nerve up.

"Can I push a button?" he asked.

"Push," I answered.

He came out behind his mother and found a button. The accordion made a sound. He pushed another button. He started grinning. He was making music.

"This is so great," he said. "Are you coming next time?"

Other people have discovered the idea of doing something for nothing, too. Depending on the time of year, there can be a steady stream of high school kids eager to volunteer at the library. Their motives are mixed. Some are idealistic and would like to leave their mark in an institution they see as somewhat fragile but deserving. Others are being practical; some guidance counselor has advised them on the salutary and invigorating effect a brief stint of volunteering will have on their college admittance form. Colleges like to see that shit—working with little kids and cleaning hypodermic needles and broken beer bottles off the beach.

For a few years my library had a sign-in sheet for volunteers that was only theoretically monitored. You signed in, went to whoever was in charge, and were given something to do. The jobs were the worst ones we had in the library: mind-numbing, repetitive, and close to unnecessary. What else do you give a high school student who is volunteering for perhaps a maximum of five hours? A kid might show up at four in the afternoon, wander around the library for an hour, and leave, having spoken to no one and having done nothing.

At the other end of the spectrum, we have people like Labelle, a young woman who has volunteered in the library for the past six years. She comes in for a half day every Tuesday and Thursday. She lives a few blocks away and walks to the library. She is quiet, serious, and never has friends come in to chat and disrupt her. Labelle is never late and never leaves early, which is even more impressive when you realize there is no penalty for this infraction. She's an unpaid volunteer; only her personal conscientiousness makes her act thus.

After a few years, Terri threw Labelle a small birthday party in the back room. There was cake, pretzels, sodas, and a card that everyone signed. Labelle was mortified by the attention but left for the day with a shy smile. After several more years, Juanita nominated Labelle for the volunteer of the year for the entire city, and she won. There was an awards banquet and Labelle was given a citation, a vigorous handshake, and a warm meal. The next time the page test was offered, Labelle took the plunge and applied. She thought it might be a mistake, because she does not do well on tests and she is not a well of self-confidence. She took it anyway and scored somewhere in the middle of about forty applicants. She knew it would not be good enough. There were too many people above her. She put it behind her and was very quiet on her Tuesdays and Thursdays. Labelle did not intend to stop doing a thing she liked to do. Six weeks later, personnel called her at home and told her to report for orientation the following Monday.

Mr. Heidenreich was much less successful in his library volunteer career. Mr. Heidenreich is in his mid-sixties and completely deaf in one ear. He began coming into the library as a patron every morning with his wife. They'd talk to the pages behind the circulation desk, talk to whoever was at reference, take out a book or two, and burn a pleasant hour. Before long, Mrs. Heidenreich put a bug in her husband's ear that he could volunteer and hang out at the library *all day long*. He was delighted with the idea. He could read stories to little kids! Tell teenagers a thing or two about life! Be a little after-school muscle!

He filled out the attendant paperwork for volunteering, even though he let us know that he thought it was a goddamn waste of time. Then he was sent to the personnel office in city hall to fill out several more forms, and there he gave the girl behind the counter a piece of his mind. By the time he was done with personnel, he had wasted a whole afternoon and he realized he was not happy at all. So he quit. He was Mrs. Heidenreich's problem again.

Chapter Fifteen
The Renaissance Patron

I AM IN THE BACK ROOM of the library, listening to a donated CD of Scott Joplin rags on our miserable portable CD player, trying to put a pile of damaged best sellers back together armed only with rubber cement and a hot glue gun designed for home crafters on a budget. It is a regular job, a job that has to be done, though not necessarily by me. A patron comes in to check out a hot new best seller, takes it home, puts it on his nightstand, and opens it up later when day is done. The book opens a little stiffly, because it is new and has never been opened before. The pages are crisp and bright white, and the cover is shiny, unmottled so far by coffee rings or trips to the beach. The patron gets comfortable in bed and opens up the book—it opens tentatively—and the patron bends the open book backward until there is a satisfying crack and the book is a little more supple, a little easier to read. The book spine has just been broken, and a broken spine means a more submissive book.

Immediately, the physics of the book are changed. It begins to slope and lean against itself, one way or the other, when it is closed. It drifts from a rectangular shape to more of a rhomboid. A small section of interior pages begins to bulge out past the hardbound cover as if it were going to seed, and these pages will tatter and discolor, eventually separating themselves completely from the rest of the book.

A broken spine in a book, especially in a public library, means the book is beginning to die. This was more rare ten or fifteen years ago, and is more common now when every aspect of a book is judged by its profitability, and the ingredients in the printing process are often of a lesser quality.

Rubber cement and hot glue—and me, incidentally—combine for an inexpensive, last-ditch effort to save a mass-market hardback book. It gives the book one last chance to be read by a few more people, if they are careful. The library knows that it is a temporary fix. We have a stamp for the inside front cover: BROKEN SPINE NOTED. It is like a bracelet worn by a diabetic. When you return the book with this message stamped inside, we know you're not the one responsible for this horrible thing. It was some other bastard before you. The book has a preexisting condition.

I only leave this pile of broken best sellers because a page has gotten on the public address system and summoned me to the front desk. There is some kind of trouble, and I am the go-to guy who is willing to be hated and vilified in the name of the library. This time, there is not one angry, argumentative patron but two, the second waiting in line right behind the first. This is always a bad thing. It means the first angry patron will have a rooting section behind him, a support group, and the second patron will finally get to the front of the line confident that the library employees are all inattentive jag-offs who screw up and do this kind of thing all the time. It is the kind of synergy large multinational companies only wish they could create.

The first patron is Mrs. Odetts. I have had words with her before. She has cautionary remarks in the "Notes" field of her computer record, but I already know this about her. She is angry, strident, petulant, indignant, all because her books are late and no one seems to want to "help" her. Helping her is a euphemism for calming her down and waiving the fines, in this case $2.25.

She has reasons, and goddamn good ones. Something to do with her husband's business flight from Aruba and how it had been rerouted due to the bad weather, the horrible weather you just have to expect in *that* part of the world. The whole thing has already been a terrible, terrible inconvenience, and now the library seems intent on profiting by the affair.

She vents for a few minutes but eventually she caves in and decides to pay the modest fines. Immediately, though, she wonders aloud why the printer at the checkout desk has not automatically printed out a receipt. She smiles and it is as if she has uncovered evidence of a second gunman in the Kennedy assassination. Mrs. Odetts is exhausting.

Behind her is a woman with a son who looks to be in his twenties. She has been unsuccessful in trying to renew his library card after a hiatus of about ten years. Bringing up the old account, I find there are two lost books outstanding, for a total of $46.38. She tells me they haven't lived in California for a while—there was a divorce, and she and her son moved to Las Vegas. Vegas wasn't the paradise she imagined, and years later they picked up again and moved back to Los Angeles.

"Isn't there a statute of limitations for things like this?" she asks with a coquettish laugh. Her son is kind of indignant and says he doesn't remember ever checking out those two books. Who would, I wonder, after ten years in another state? Even I'm surprised the books are still listed on her account, but I'm not ready to get rid of the fines simply because they are embarrassing. Waiving overdue fines is one thing—as long as we get the book back we're more or less happy. Lost books are a little more serious.

After both crises are resolved, I am on the way back to the hot-glue gun when a woman stops and asks me about remodeling a bathroom. Her name is Lydia. Everyone knows this because she is a regular and her name is on her lapel, a smiling picture ID from the hospital where she works.

What do you think, she asks me, galvanized or copper? After being stunned at the first few estimates, she plans to read up and do the thing herself. Who's got that kind of money? she laughs. I know! she tells me. Plumbers!

Lydia is in her late fifties, maybe in her sixties. She is Irish, and every time I see her her outlook and demeanor are pleasant. Her hair is close-cropped, bright red, giving her a kind of punk look, but she says it is responsible for getting her out of the house fifteen minutes earlier every morning. She doesn't need to look at herself in the mirror to know what's going on with her hair. "I already know what I look like," she says. "Yikes." She leaves the house and walks to the corner where she catches a bus to her job at the UCLA Medical Center, where she works in the AIDS hospice there. She used to have a car, but with maintenance, upkeep, gas, and insurance, it gobbled up too much money. She got rid of it.

"I check out these stupid Janet Evanovich novels to read on the bus," she cackles, jarring several nearby patrons. "All I have to do is open the book and I don't have to chat with the crazy people, simple as that. They leave me alone!"

I give Lydia my opinion on home-improvement projects as far as galvanized vs. copper—it's copper. More important than this, though, I tell her to hire someone who knows what doing. I confess to Lydia that I always wind up doing the same damn home-improvement project twice. I do it the first time, realize the mistakes I've been making about 80 percent of the way through, and then I rip it out and start all over again. Yes, certain things you should leave to the pros.

Lydia disagrees completely. "I can stick my head underneath the kitchen sink with a flashlight and save a few hundred bucks, or I can sit on the sofa and eat buttered popcorn and watch television. Please. Shoot me now. Have you *watched* television lately?"

So she takes the books home and puts in a sink and a commode. It takes her one attempt.

"Any problems?" I ask her some weeks later when she returns the books.

"Problems?" she says and takes off her glasses. "Yes. I'm getting old." But the plumbing fixtures were a piece of cake.

The next time she comes in she needs a bunch of books on dog training. One of the young men in the AIDS hospice has died and left behind a puppy. The puppy seems to be a rottweiler–pit bull mix, and whatever it is he's going to be a big one. Her coworkers were going to take the pup to the animal shelter, but Lydia took it home instead. The young man who passed away had been in the hospice for seven months and was one of her favorites. The puppy will be a nice remembrance, even if he never stops chewing on the furniture.

When her books come back overdue, she pays the fines on the same day. If she loses a book, she pays for the lost book. "It's the *library*, for god's sake," she says in explanation. "Let's be a little responsible," she says to the startled patron behind her in line. "Right?"

Lydia is one of a handful of patrons who use the entire library, not just a small part of it. She takes out books on remodeling, Thai cooking, estate planning, aromatherapy, biographies on Princess Di and Richard Burton, outdoor landscaping, photography, container gardening, quilting, genealogy, histories of the Civil War, rose cultivation, résumé writing and interviewing, home composting techniques, and a variety of other topics. Some patrons use books as an aid to sleep. Lydia uses books to make her world larger. She is happy with her small successes and not overwhelmed or crushed by occasional failure. She says that working with AIDS patients has changed her perspective somewhat. It has hardened her where she had been soft, and made her soft where she had been hard. One of her library friends confessed that she didn't think she could ever work where Lydia worked, she could never do what Lydia does. Lydia answered, "Sure you could. Sure you could. You'd be surprised. You just get caught up at times, but you could do it. You have to. People need help. Christ."

Last spring, Lydia finds me at the reference desk and shows me the cover of a weekly national magazine. There are several AIDS activists being hauled away by the police. It looks like the streets of Paris or New York, and there are men in riot gear, batons, large snarling dogs, and what looks like tear gas canisters sailing through the air. She points to a young man in the middle of the picture. He is thin, has a light beard, and is wearing a flannel shirt. She is gleaming with pride.

"That's David—David! My son! He moved out of California years ago. What a mess. We would argue about his illness—it was a lot of frustration on both our parts. When he found out he had HIV, he was going to stay well by drinking pomegranate juice and doing some kind of yoga. Fresh air and deep breathing exercises. Right. Then he started getting sick the first time and figured he ought to listen to what the doctors were telling him.

"When he started getting better—the first time—he almost went off the medicine and went back to the pomegranate juice. I told him, Davie, honey, don't fool around like this with your health. You want to stay well, stay on the medication. Drink the juice, too, if you want, but stay on the medication. Oh, he's seen a lot of his friends die. All of them young—so terribly young."

Lydia raps the picture once with her finger. "He's very articulate when he's angry," she says with a smile and no little amount of pride.

Underneath her arm, she has a book on chair upholstery; she thinks she will take a whack at it. What's the worst that can happen? She'll have an ugly chair. Well, she has one now. But her world will be bigger still. Who knows, maybe it won't turn out so bad. Maybe the chair will wind up tall and straight and handsome and it will be the kind of chair a person would admire and want to sit in. She also has a book on growing tomatoes and other vegetables, a thick volume on pharmacology, and an old mystery by Agatha Christie—for the crazy people on the bus, she laughs, in a way that makes you want to laugh, too. Then she leaves the library and prepares to catch the bus that takes her to work.

Chapter Sixteen
Card Registrations

TERRI CAME BACK TO WORK a week after the marmoset incident wearing high-collared, long-sleeve shirts and pants, not wanting to be a graphic poster girl for the Effects of Allergic Reactions to the Skin. The cause of her ailment was never determined, but all of the other children's librarians knew it had something to do with "Kathy's Animal Friends," so Kathy did no repeat business with the city. Marmoset, schmarmoset, the animals were a smoking gun. When no other children came down with the affliction, city administration breathed a huge sigh of relief. They had contained the outbreak.

For the first few days, Terri was very tentative, expecting to be laid low once again by the same mystery bug. Once again, her OCD was a valuable aid. She passed out a sheet of paper to every full-time employee listing her symptoms, her husband's cell phone number, the phone number of the nearest emergency room, her allergist's office number and his home number, and an accompanying Mapquest route to the emergency room printed out from the Internet. She also had her sisters' cell phone numbers and asked us to notify them when she keeled over. They had their own sheets of paper.

When Mr. Weams and his janitorial crew came in the second morning she was back to empty the trash cans and light up the public restrooms with their chemicals, Terri gave them all thank-you cards. Mr.

Weams was speechless. This, apparently, was the way he always thought he deserved to be treated. He told her if she ever decided to leave her husband, damn it, he would be there for her consideration. Terri was simultaneously touched and weirded out by the gesture.

The thing is, she knew she had to come back when she did. The library was gearing up for its annual registration drive in the local elementary schools. It is a big deal. Getting a library card is a kid's first taste of freedom and responsibility. Take books out, bring them back, and all is well. The system works. A library card is not like an adjustable rate mortgage where three years down the road you are going to be sitting at the kitchen table saying, "How in god's name did my kid ever get sucked into this?" The library is not meant to generate income, or even break even. It was created to consistently lose money—slowly, evenly, into the foreseeable future.

So they make it relatively easy to get a library card.

During the card registration drive, second graders come into the library with their class, hand us a form that has been more or less filled out, and we treat the information as though it were all true. The parents are not there. They are just signatures on the bottom of the brief form. We do not really require verification. The feeling is, however, that most parents know that a library card is a good thing, and the parents will do what parents are supposed to do—step up and do the right thing when their child loses a book, drops the book into the toilet, or leaves the book in the hamster cage overnight.

Legally, they aren't required to give us a great deal of information: a home address, a phone number, a driver's license if they'd like to show it to us. But some people are screwed up. They will make up addresses; they will say they have no phone, no driver's license. The less information you have on them, the less able you are to get a hold of them when the books drift overdue and cruise into lost territory.

Some patrons put down post office boxes as their home address. This is not a happy thing, because when the patron has $750 worth of missing books it is impossible to knock on their post office box and ask them politely where the books are. At this point, they are gone. But if the DMV puts the post office box on their driver's license, it's good enough for us. If it is not on their driver's license we are dubious.

"I can't get mail where I live."

This statement, too, makes us suspect, because as far as we know the mail goes everywhere. When we are lied to in the first tentative moments of the relationship, we know it will end in tears, accusations, and large fines.

A library card application may be crammed with so many, well, lies that the whole process comes to a complete stop. On one application, it says the card is for Donna Mae Denker. There are four other Donna Mae Denkers in the system. Their birthdays are close, their addresses strikingly similar, but no, they must be other Donna Mae Denkers. There are large fines on each of Donna Mae Denker's cards. Hundreds of dollars. The Donna Mae Denker in front of you is incredulous, and amazed that there is at least one more Donna Mae Denker in the world and that she is such a scamp. She scrunches up her face in sincere befuddlement, thinking for a moment.

Wait a minute.

She has just the thing in her car that will clear this whole mess up. She walks out to her car, gets inside, starts the engine, and pulls out of the parking lot. She has, in her own way, cleared it all up.

Two weeks later, she will come into another library and try it again. Two months later, she may come back into another library and try it again. If caught, she will be astounded and a little bit angry that someone is running roughshod over her good name. If she is not caught, Donna Mae Denker gets to burn another card.

Earlier this month, a woman comes into the library and says she would like to get a new library card. Her purse has been stolen and she wants to cancel out the old card. But there are four lost books on her old card. No big deal, as they're children's paperbacks, but still they'll have to be replaced. The books have been on her card for two and a half years.

When was her purse stolen?

"Why," she says, thinking quickly, "Two and a half years ago." The person who stole her purse must have come to the library short-ly after he stole her purse—and used the library card! That's what happened! It is so ridiculous I am speechless. Even her elementary school–age children roll their eyes and tell their mother they'll be waiting by the front door. They are trying to create some aesthetic distance from the impending train wreck.

Things get progressively worse when I look up her son's name, who has standing fines of $64.

And then she remembers a few more details.

"My son has never had a library card! This *is* someone else! Whoever stole my purse must have done this!"

I cannot argue. It's too complicated to argue. Her story is chang-ing, slowly and dramatically, like pack ice in the spring. Eventually, she complains that she is not used to this kind of treatment, and out she goes in a huff.

Another patron was stunned that she needed a library card at all. She showed me a fistful of other cards she already had just to illustrate how ridiculous it all was. Couldn't one of these work? Maybe an ATM card, a supermarket card? Aren't they all somehow linked together in some way, through some gigantic, throbbing, underground, super-cooled facility? They had to be. That was the only thing that made sense to her. I told her it might be going that way, but not yet, not yet.

We keep the signed library card applications for almost a year. Then we send them to the main branch and have them shredded. At this point, the paperwork is all gone and the records are stored com-pletely electronically. When the power surges and fails, as it has every summer since Ken Lay began to really appreciate golden bathroom fixtures, there are no records at all for a while. People hand us library cards and we write the numbers down, along with the numbers of the books they are checking out. Hours or days later when the power is restored, we find we have checked out books to people who have completely fallen out of the system. Their records are gone. We don't know their names, their addresses, their phone numbers, or anything else about them. And when they bring the books back, there is no patron record to take the books off of — the books are just back.

The grand prize winner of card application fraud and excess goes to a woman who is about thirty-five, white, a little heavy, and has an astonishing assortment of bracelets, rings, chains, and charms on her wrists, none of which appear to be expensive. She is at the reference desk and asks about the procedure for getting a library card.

Has she had a library card before?

"Why, no," she says.

She fills out a library card application under the name of Angelica Williams. The information is keyed into the computer and the computer kicks it back, rejecting it. Angelica Williams already has a card. The woman smiles patiently and says, "No, huh-uh, that's not me." And a good thing, too. The other Angelica William's library card is blocked with three lost library books from a few years back and an attendant debt of more than $70.

We show her the record on the computer screen. She shakes her head. She's never heard of these three books, and *that* is not her address.

No problem, we tell her. What the hell, two people with the same name — in Los Angeles? Wow, what a coincidence.

This problem is not limited to the John Smiths of the world. In my library it is Lin Ying, Francis Nguyen, Maria Martinez, and Jose Gutierrez. Every nationality has a handful of its own John Smiths. It is easier to abandon your ethnic identity than the name that symbolizes it. When a John Kleshinski wants to know about this *other* John Kleshinski in the system, only a small part of it is a proprietary fear — most of it is curiosity. There's another one of *me* out there?

The first clue on the Angelica Williams account came when I later examined both records at the same time, which is one of the things I do. One Angelica Williams lived at 1322 Oak Street, the other lived at 1327 Oak Street. Just about across the street from each other.

I believe in coincidence. I believe that this kind of thing happens all the time, and it is only because we are not made aware of all the particulars that we are not continually astonished. Once in college, I hitchhiked from Ohio State University in Columbus, Ohio, to Ohio University in Athens, Ohio, to visit a girlfriend of mine from high school. I had no idea where she lived. I only had a phone number. When my ride dropped me off near the university, I found a dormitory, went to a room on the first floor, and asked to use their phone so I could call the girl. Wisely, the girls in the room didn't quite trust me. They said, give us the phone number through the door and we'll call her for you. I gave them the number and they closed the door while I waited in the hall for them to put the call through. A girl finally opened the door with a puzzled look on her face. She said, "That's our number. Who are you trying to call?"

"Loree," I said.

The girl turned and shouted, "Loree! There's a guy here to see you!"

I had squandered all of my Vegas and lottery good fortune finding a semi-girlfriend in Athens, Ohio—and she wasn't that thrilled to see me.

Just as Loree's roommate didn't trust me, I didn't trust Angelica Williams. I called her, asked her a few questions, and she admitted that Angelica Williams was her married name. Her real name, her maiden name, was Angelica Ramsay. Those lost books had been taken out by her no-good ex-husband. It wasn't really fair, she said, but all right, she'd make good on those lost books. Say ten dollars every time she came in to use the library. She just wanted to check out some picture books for her baby.

Lillian the senior librarian heard the words "books," "for," and "baby" and it was all over. We love this stuff. We love giving second chances to people who have been dumped at the shit end of the economic spectrum. Rich people don't have the time or need to invest in the same kind of bullshit, and they use the library in a different way. Rich people will buy the best seller, read it, and donate it to the library when they're done. Rich people don't go to a book for advice on an important matter, either. They'll make an appointment with an adviser. When rich people fuck up and lose a book, they grumble and eventually pay for it. Poor people have to dance, or slip and fall on the way out and threaten to sue.

We gave Angelica Ramsay a second library card, urged her to clean up the first one as soon as she could, and felt very warm and toasty about ourselves. We were the Man. We were doing good deeds. Best of all, we weren't doing it with our own money. Angelica Ramsay took out six books—two picture books for a child, two books on doing the paperwork on your own divorce in California, and two general books of adult fiction. The books stayed out for several months, long enough to be considered lost, and when we called the number she supplied to remind her about the books the phone had been disconnected.

Hell.

Well, you expect that in a public library. That kind of behavior is ensured in a certain small percentage of the population. We call and make our empty threats, if the phone has not been disconnected, and then we move on.

Five years later, a woman comes into the library and walks up to the reference desk. She would like to get a library card. Is it her first one? Why, yes. And while she's here, she would like to get library cards for her three sons. They are waiting outside in the van, probably asleep. She really doesn't want to wake them up. The forms are all filled out. Her children have already signed the forms, which we require, although we know full well that a juvenile can't enter into a legally binding contract. They can't go out and buy refrigerators and plasma screen televisions. They can't cosign for a car. Their signatures mean nothing in a court of law. But we require it because we believe . . . hell, I'm at a loss to tell you what we believe. I don't know why we require it. I guess it's like college hazing rituals. It's certainly illegal, but that's the way we've always done it. It's a tradition. We're fiddling on the roof.

The feel-good answer is that the child feels more responsible by doing such a grown-up thing, and will therefore be a much more mature patron. But it's not like we're relying on scientific studies. It just feels like a good answer.

So we give the woman, Angelica Dashell, four library cards, one for her and three for the children we have never seen in her van. She takes out four books on her card and leaves. Later on, as I enter the full registration into the computer, I get the Big Surprise. Angelica Williams was Angelica Ramsay and now she is Angelica Dashell. Angelica had married several times, and every time she did so she took out a library card under her new name. Each time she started out fresh, but each time she made the same mistakes, including losing a handful of library books.

I knew exactly what to do—lock up every one of the new library accounts and just hope to god the books came back. Lillian, however, cringed at my decision. It was wrong to ostracize children from the library. It flew in the face of every library virtue she had ever written about in graduate school. If these Dashell kids ever hoped to have a chance in life, someone had to cut them some slack. Someone had to take a chance, and Lillian was just the person to do it. So we locked up Angelica Williams/Angelica Ramsay/Angelica Dashell, but approved the three cards for her sons. On the notes field of each card in the computer, we put the warning JUVENILE MATERIALS ONLY. This is not in accord with library policy, because anyone can check out anything in a public library. But we put it in anyway. Lillian had gotten used to making the big decisions.

That fall when school came back into session, we met the rest of the family.

Ansel Ramsay is fifteen years old and has recently been given to his grandparents, who live in the same approximate area. Angelica lived in a

hotel room with her boys, and the grandparents adopted Ansel as a kindness. Ansel comes into the library every day after high school and tries to
keep his half brothers in line. Nathan Dashell is twelve, racially mixed,
and doesn't need his older brother's fucking help. He tells Ansel he can
take care of himself. But he is really just a child—he threatens to dole
out impressive violence from a heavy bicycle chain one minute and is
in tears fifteen minutes later because some old woman shushed him and
accused him, wrongly! of excessive noise. And Nathan is very protective
of his eight-year-old half brother, Thad. Thad has the face of a sweet,
pudgy angel and he wants to be good, but the odds on him are long.

They get to the library at 3:15 p.m. every afternoon and are
picked up just before closing time, 8 p.m., every night, unless Mom
forgets or is running late. So the schedule is: a full day at school and
then five hours of tedium at the library. This is brutal. They come in,
chat with their buds, use the Internet and play a few games, hang out
in the library parking lot and maybe throw pinecones or rocks at some
cars, come back in, do a little homework, and it's still just 4:30 p.m.

Their friends are all picked up by five, the library begins to empty
out, and there are still three hours left to burn. Ansel leaves the library at
six and warns his siblings not to fuck up. By 6:15 p.m., Nathan is ready
to do something, anything, but the options are all bad. He can leave his
little brother by himself and go play out in the dark, which is kind of
cool, but he looks back at the library from the dark and sees Thad inside,
peering out into the blackness, trying to see what his brother is doing.
He can walk back to the school and see if there's any doors or windows
unlocked, but it's gotten dangerous there. He tells us no way will he go
exploring there again after dark. One of the young black janitors chased
him down recently, grabbed him by the shirt, and threatened to do a
number on him if he ever came back. Nathan has been beaten by adults
a few times and does not like it. They never quit when it's time to quit.
Getting punched in the face by an angry, two-hundred-pound man is a
whole different thing than getting bitch-slapped by someone the same
age, like one of his brothers. It does not compare.

He could hang out in the bushes next to the library and Thad would know he's there, close by. Pop out of the bushes at opportune moments and try the car doors as the patrons browsed for books inside. Throw rocks at the streetlights. If he gets too bored, or if it's raining, he can go inside and play hide-and-seek with his brother, which he sees as a kind of noble, brotherly chore. He can pull the leaves off the houseplants that Lillian is trying to grow by the back windows of the library. He can tear pictures from the teen magazines to decorate his wall at home. He can make loud noises. Or he can fuck with the few remaining latchkey kids still stuck at the library and make sure they remember who he is.

Thad only knows that the library is more fun, and more forgiving, than Mom's hotel room. In the hotel room he wears headphones and listens to rap to blot out Mom's television shows. He also keeps his headphones on so he doesn't have to listen to any of her boyfriends. Sometimes when Mom and her boyfriend are sitting on the bed, drinking beer, watching television, they get really loud, so he turns to the wall and cranks up the volume on his headphones until it is his whole world. For this reason, he says matter-of-factly, he likes to keep his headphones working, the battery charged up. He lends them to no one, not even his brothers.

Thad gets into an inordinate number of fights at school and at the library, and perhaps part of it is because his brothers are always there to defend him, like a small army in reserve. When one fights, they all fight, and when things are slow they often wind up fighting each other.

Nathan and Thad wind up on the floor of the library, rolling around, laughing and spitting and slapping at each other, and Lillian the senior librarian makes them sit at different tables. Throwing an eight-year-old out into the dark seems wrong, especially when there is a definite chill in the air and a fine rain is falling, and Lillian is hesitant to do so. They have nowhere else to go. Thrown out of the library, they sit under whatever protection they can find and look at every pair of headlights entering the parking lot, hoping that this is one of those days when Mom comes in a little early—because it is dark and raining and cold, and because she knows they get thrown out almost every day.

Lillian the senior librarian has a quiet hope that a simple talk with Mom will do the trick, and she stays late one night and invites Mrs. Dashell into her office for a heart-to-heart. Angelica knows how to play off Lillian's cues. Lillian is worried, yes, Angelica is worried, too. Lillian is frustrated. Hey, me too, Angelica says with a commiserating, worldly laugh. They're quite a handful. Lillian is congenial and reaching out, they make extended eye contact, and at the end, yes, Angelica is so glad we had this little talk. They both walk out of the office relieved, but for different reasons. Lillian does not even feel remotely conned until she tells us this story the following morning. And then it seems obvious.

Of course, nothing changes, not even a little. The boys are thrown out for theft, vandalism, fighting, almost every day. Lillian's next step is calling the Community Lead Officer for the school district. The Community Lead Officer is a Bay City policeman. His job is to watch over a group of schools, paying attention to everything that goes on. By this kind of concentration, he is able to recognize trends, and recognize faces. The current CLO knows all about Ansel and Nathan and Thad. Frankly, he is tired of dealing with them. He spends too much of every day writing reports and visiting teachers and calling social workers and making what sounds like empty threats to Angelica Dashell.

He tells Terri and Lillian that talking to Angelica Dashell is like lecturing a German shepherd. Their ears go back and they act contrite while you're talking to them, and as soon as you're done they bound off to dig up your rosebushes. He wishes she would move in the middle of the night and clear up all his problems, once and for all. He hopes that she will remember to take her boys. If she doesn't, it creates another mountain of paperwork.

But the family stays put. Although we do not like dealing with the Dashells/Ramsays every day, we get used to it, but it is like getting used to a permanent physical disability. It is relentlessly frustrating, and soon we don't know when it was any different.

Next September, when school starts again, they are still here. Angelica has not moved in the middle of the night. Now, however, there are two big differences. The boys are taller and larger than they were the year before, and Nathan is now as tall as Lillian. This year, it will be like correcting and shushing a trio of raptors from *Jurassic Park*. And Angelica is once again pregnant.

A few of the library employees threaten to quit unless something is done, but no one, including the police, seems to know what can be done. On the third week of the new semester there is an unprecedented meeting in the library. There are school administrators from two different schools, two patrolmen who have been involved in incidents, the Community Lead Officer, a teacher, a social worker of indeterminate standing, and three employees from the library.

The social worker comes up with a surefire idea. She can enroll all three children in after-school activities at the local YMCA, and her department will pick up 90 percent of the cost. They'll still wind up coming to the library, but not until after 6:30 p.m.. The Y should be able to burn off their extra energy.

It is a great idea but it doesn't work. They get in trouble at the YMCA, and Angelica resists coming up with her 10 percent. Three weeks later they're all ours again.

By November, even library administration has had enough. Nathan and Thad were playing tag in the parking lot, it turned into slap and kick boxing, one of Thad's friends tried to break them up, and Nathan wound up choking him out with his bicycle chain. All three of them are permanently banned from the library. If we see them in the library, lurking in the bushes outside the library, or anywhere near the library, we are instructed to call the police. The police will then drive over to Angelica's hotel room and arrest them all as they show up. The police also warn us that if we relent and let the boys back in the library, even for an emergency pee, we are back to square one.

Angelica Williams/Ramsay/Dashell has outstanding fines for lost books totaling $267. Nathan and Thad have lost books and CDs on their records totaling $600. Ansel still has a card. Life with his grandparents has been good.

Ansel has a girlfriend and a small role in the senior play. He has given his girlfriend a promise ring, which he explains is a preengagement engagement ring. He has a job for two hours every night after school bagging groceries and has used some of his earnings to buy himself a personal computer. He says he would like to be a film editor after high school, and that he is wicked talented in this area. He does not hear from his brothers much. His grandparents have forbidden their daughter from coming to their house, and Ansel feels badly, personally responsible for failing his brothers, and he wishes he could have done more.

A year later, I am working at the circulation desk at the main library when Angelica comes up to the desk with a baby in her arms and asks for an application. I am talking to another patron but I recognize the voice and the accent. She fills out an application under the name Angelica Marquez, and when she is asked if she has ever had a card before, she smiles, rocks her baby lovingly, and says, "Why, no."

Chapter Seventeen
Cinco de Mayo

SCHOOL HAS BEEN OUT for more than an hour, we are all out on the floor manning our posts, when Juanita gets my attention from across the library. She is making big windmill motions with her arms, which is shorthand for "Come here now!" As I walk to the front of the library, she increases the spin on her windmilling, as if she is approaching take-off speed, which I think means, "Hurry!" As I arrive, she points to two tall, black middle-school boys who have just walked out the front door. They seem physically mature and might even be in high school. Neither are regulars, and they hook up with a larger contingent in the middle of the parking lot. Occasionally, they glance toward the front door of the library to see if anyone else is following them.

"Something's not right," Juanita says with some alarm. "I don't recognize any of those kids. And none of them are carrying books. They've already been home and dumped them. This smells like a fight. You think?"

I don't know what to think. The kids in the parking lot are sure acting like *something's* going to happen in a minute or two, but a library parking lot seems like a stupid place to schedule such an event. And I don't see whom they're planning to fight with.

The two kids are impatient and come back into the library. Juanita greets them by the front door.

"Hi! How you guys doing today? Can I help either of you find something?"

"Hey," they answer weakly. "Just looking."

"Well, you let me know if you need anything," Juanita says.

They drift into the library and disappear into the stacks. "Walk with me!" Juanita whispers, and we tail them into the library. They wind up standing in front of two Latino kids who are also not regulars, but at least they have books open in front of them. The black kids are gesturing, smiling, posing, and the net conversation is that they would like the two Latinos to follow them outside. Fight-wise, every-one seems to be on the same page.

Both the Latino kids have cell phones in their hands, and I as-sume that they have called in reinforcements—friends, brothers, who-ever they can muster up.

Juanita inserts herself into the mix. "Okay, you two standing up will have to find some seats. Now. Or I'm going to be calling some par-ents." Sometimes this threat works. Sometimes they find it amusing.

"We going," one of the black kids says, and follows it with, "You coming?"

Juanita senses that there will be a lull of at least a few minutes before there are any real fireworks and tells me to ask Terri to call the police complaint line and tell them there's going to be a fight in front of the library. Then she tells me to grab the camera from the back room and meet her by the front door. When things start happening, we will take candid shots of the participants and show them to the local principals so they can mete out what we hope will be richly deserved punishment.

When I meet her again by the front door, she has pulled *The Clan of the Cave Bear* off the shelves. It is a nice, six-hundred-page book that can be used both recreationally and defensively. Then we walk outside and stand with the other spectators. Our presence is poi-son. We are making everyone else feel awkward.

Just as the two Latino boys step outside to continue the ramped-up posturing, three cars pull up in front of the library, filled with friends and relatives of the Latino kids—large ones—and, most importantly, one of the boy's fathers.

All the father says is "Get in the car" and the fight is over, the situation defused. The father nods briefly at Juanita, and Juanita nods back. The two black kids are not going to get mouthy against this kind of opposition. Both sides withdraw, the crowd evaporates like soap bubbles on hot cement, and when a patrol car finally pulls up the parking lot is calm and empty. Juanita invites the patrolmen inside for a cup of coffee and some cherry walnut pastries that a patron has brought in for us, and they confide that a lot of weird stuff has been happening lately—and it's all because of Cinco de Mayo.

Cinco de Mayo, May fifth, is Mexican Independence Day. It's a big deal, there's nostalgia, people wave the Mexican flag, and there's a parade somewhere in the city. In the Los Angeles area, the American gringo can celebrate right next to his Mexican brother by having a Corona and/or a shot of tequila. And for most people that's all there is to it. The day comes and goes, there's a mention on the 11 o'clock news, and the next morning we can all root around for something else to hold our attention for fourteen minutes until the next thing blows up.

For the past few years, however, Cinco de Mayo has had problems. It has come to represent some kind of amorphous, unnamed strife and animosity between Latinos and blacks, mostly in areas with large blocs of these populations. The Latino kids walk together down the halls. The black kids walk down the same halls. Anyone with large balls and a flair for drama can light the fuse in almost any school. Seems like hating the white man could have united the two groups in a common cause, but lately it's just not good enough. It's lost cachet.

We're not sure what to expect in the libraries, and the e-mails from administration would like us to believe that it's all a bunch of silly, unfounded rumors—and why shouldn't it be? Los Angeles has a large, diverse population, and Latinos and blacks are only a part of the mix. We have Indians, Afghans, Pakistanis, and Muslims and Buddhists, even a smattering of Sikhs. We have a thin contingent of people from Bangladesh, the country that seems to be under water several months of the year. We have Japanese, Chinese, and Koreans. The Japanese distrust the Chinese, the Chinese despise the Japanese, and the only thing they can agree on is their utter contempt for the Koreans. The Koreans are the Irish of the twenty-first century. The white folks also come in flavors—all the way from garishly affluent to hideously white trash. But white folk are a small isle surrounded by color in Los Angeles.

The Samoans are undoubtedly one of the toughest groups around, but their numbers are slim. There just aren't many of them around. When I worked at an all-night technical typing agency in Carson, California, one year, all of the other typists were Samoan. When we took our fifteen-minute break at 3 a.m., they would all pull their chairs away from the desks, lie on the floor with their heads underneath the desks, and sleep until rousted by the office supervisor. The best typist in the group was a homosexual Samoan named Ulai. He was six feet, five inches tall with big hair, and he weighed about 250. He wore short shorts and Hawaiian shirts tied and knotted so you could see his waist. He was going for petite.

One night he came into the agency flushed, crying. A group of men in a car threw a Coke at him and called him a fag as he was crossing the street. Four men got out of the car, jumped him, and he beat the hell out of all of them, until they jumped back into their car and drove away. Ulai's shirt was torn. He had broken one of his lovely painted nails. His hair was leaning to the side. Kicking serious ass had destroyed his poise.

Then there are the black folk, but this is the white-bread suburbs, not South Central Los Angeles, so any jive is something imported or picked up from television, not the streets. The whites are just an oh-so-special minority, because they remember the days when they were totally in charge.

The Latinos haven't come together as a voting presence yet, but they will, they will. Their numbers alone are impressive. As a graph trying to express population growth, their lines shoot off the charts. If Latinos were a stock, we would all want some.

For several weeks prior to Cinco de Mayo, we've heard a number of rumors. News reports on the radio. There's going to be a race-inspired gang war. A black street gang of old-timers hijacked a shipment of drugs intended for distribution by the Mexican mafia, and payback is supposed to entail dead black schoolkids. The kids will be shot from cars as they walk to school, and they will all be wearing white T-shirts. Or it will happen on the freeway, car-to-car. The news channels run the stories, run the rumors, run the denial of the rumors, so it must be true. It all feeds the flame. Obviously, something's going on. Looks like we will find out exactly what on Cinco de Mayo.

On the radio, the local talk shows drone on endlessly about Cinco de Mayo. They appreciate a topic that hasn't already been driven into the ground. It's a rumor given too much air time. Utter nonsense. It couldn't possibly be true.

On the other hand, "Y'all will see. We will burn this town to the ground."

And so on.

My youngest daughter goes to a high school on the L.A. strip, a long, thin piece of land that extends from the middle of downtown all the way to the harbor in San Pedro, thus turning Los Angeles into a port. It is a freakish, unnatural boundary, a phallus that wends its way to the ocean, and it is a no-man's-land that adjacent communities are only too happy to ignore. Call 911 on the Bay City side of the street and the cops are there in moments. Depending on the call, there may be multiple units, dogs, and helicopters that will light up your front yard like a new car dealership. Have the same emergency on the Los Angeles strip side of the street and it will take hours for any kind of response. The streets will stay dark and quiet and forgotten. Different jurisdictions, different street signs, different police cars, and different rules. Even the homeless are wise to the differences. They panhandle on the L.A. strip side of the street. If they forget, the Bay City police will remind them, and roughly.

My daughter's high school is in the L.A. strip. They have a football team, guidance counselors, a school newspaper, cheerleaders, a drama department, an orchestra, security guards, a number of assistant principals, and a chain-link fence that secures the perimeter of the school. The fence is to protect the school from bad influences in the community, and to protect the community from bad influences in the school. More often than not, the bad influences seep out, not in.

There are gang members in the school population, but my daughter does not feel as if she is in any danger. My daughter is a white girl in a school where white girls comprise about 3 percent of the student population. Her friends are part of different groups. She does not have a racial agenda, and she knows, as does everyone else, which groups to lean away from. She does not want to worry us, and so she does not tell us about the racial tension and the posturing and the fights that are as common as the seagulls in back of the school next to the cafeteria Dumpsters.

Even my daughter is concerned about Cinco de Mayo. The rumors are sweeping back and forth across the school like brushfires. It's going to happen at a certain time. Automatic weapons are crammed into lockers. Someone is going to die. Carloads of gangbangers from San Pedro are going to import mayhem. The black kids are going to wear different-colored armbands, like Homeland Security, and the colors will symbolize different messages.

Peace.

Community.

Stand united.

An eye for an eye.

Never again.

First strike.

Of course, in the library, the regular patrons are fairly oblivious to this approaching storm. It is a problem that will manifest itself somewhere else. We will read about shots fired, see the picture in the newspaper of blood spilled, friends weeping with outrage, holding pathetic little bouquets of ruined flowers, but it is a distant land. Not here. Not in the library.

One of the regulars, Little Tilafaiiga, comes in with his son, and he makes brief eye contact. Less than two seconds. From my retail days, I know that when a person makes eye contact in a business, either that person wants to ask you a question or they're about to do something on the level of shoplifting and they want to see if you notice them. If you return the two-second gaze, it means: I absolutely see you and know what you're going to do. I will remember your face.

Little Tilafaiiga makes eye contact. He is with his son.

He wants to talk.

Little Tilafaiiga is Samoan, easily over 350 pounds. He has tribal tattoos that ring his sizable biceps, he is obviously a weight lifter, obviously a man not to be fucked with. Little Tilafaiiga is a volunteer coach at one of the high schools. He has set up and now maintains a weight-training course for student athletes. He knows the machines, knows how to train, how to do the reps and how many to do. Of course, he would love it if they picked him up as a part-time employee and actually cut him a regular check, but for now he's doing it for free. He is also an officer at a juvenile facility in downtown Los Angeles and works with "youthful offenders" who for the most part want nothing at all to do with his stupid weight-training program. These are juveniles who have jumped into street gangs, juveniles with baby faces who have already fucked and seen death and pulled triggers and gotten drunk at a friend's funeral.

Little Tilafaiiga moves a little slower than you think he should, and I think he moves slowly because it gives him time to wipe the emotion out of his face and the judgment out of his eyes. Still, he stands over his son and tells him, no, he may not go outside and hang with his classmates until he can prove his homework is done.

After addressing his son's homework situation, he takes me aside and asks me what I've heard about May fifth. In the juvenile facility, it's the big topic. With the police on the other side of the glass, it's *the* big topic. In a sincere, quiet voice, he urges me to look out for my kids on the fifth. Even if 85 percent of the talk is just crazy bullshit swagger, there is a resonance in the remaining 15 percent that cannot be ignored. Something is going to happen. Some stupid, preventable thing. And when that thing happens, all the rest of it is going to happen too.

Little Tilafaiiga's son, who is a handsome, scrawny kid with conservative hair, about eight inches taller and two hundred pounds lighter than his father, looks up from his eighth-grade math book and Little Tilafaiiga glowers, his face condensing into absolute seriousness, and he says, quietly, "Keep studying. I want to see your homework when you're done." His son groans and sinks back into his math homework. He is not worried. None of the kids are worried. A lot of the parents are not worried, either.

The police are worried, though. School administrators are worried. Little Tilafaiiga is worried. And with this kind of lineage I am worried, too. We are worried about our children, that they might be accidentally shot for going to school and being in the wrong place on May fifth.

On the morning of May fifth, we get a few e-mails at the library that tell us the city's official position on gangbanging, loaded automatic weapons, and potential race war. The city is unequivocally against it. It is overcast and cloudy outside, cool enough to wear a long-sleeved shirt, which is good. It is not race war weather.

The crowds in the library are unusually thin after school, and we all think it's because parents are picking up their kids as soon as school gets out. There were a few fistfights at my daughter's school, but things were broken up quickly and economically. Administration came in early, stayed late, wore walkie-talkies all day long, and kept in constant touch with the police, many of whom sat in squad cars ringing the high school campus.

News helicopters that had been waiting for trouble to break out at the high schools were eventually rerouted to the 405 freeway where an overturned gasoline tanker closed traffic in both directions and smoldered until it was covered in foam and consecrated on the evening news.

Several days later, my daughter told me that 1,600 black and Latino students called in sick on May fifth. Almost 40 percent of the whole school. The 1,600 missing students helped the day to go by unremarkably. Few fights, zero gunplay, no bloodshed. Administration was mighty proud, and several administrators were written up for their skill in dealing with the half-empty school.

Cinco de Mayo.

We can all breathe easy.

Until next year.

Chapter Eighteen
MMM

THE LIBRARY WOULD LIKE TO HAVE some kind of insider, hip patois, but we don't. If we knew there was some kind of inner-circle lingo that identified us as librarians, we'd resist it. The closest thing we have to a specialized language is saying "circ" when we mean how many times a book has checked out, as in, "That book by Janet Evanovich has circ'd fifteen times in the last three months. Maybe we should get a second copy."

There's also a thing called "weeding." Weeding means going through the library and getting the books off the shelves that are no longer pulling their weight. The public is always stunned when they learn that a public library periodically and rigorously pulls books off the shelves and either sells them for a few bucks or throws them away. They think we treat each book like an eternal flame. If we did that, however, we'd quickly run out of room and have to stop buying new books. Then where would we be? So we weed.

The one special phrase that we all know about, and you don't, is MMM. It is our one phrase that means heads-up, take cover, incoming, code blue, May Day, and shots fired, all in one. It works like this. A patron comes in to check out a book. We swipe in their library card, and that person's information becomes available on a computer screen. Address. Phone number. Driver's license. Birthdate. Preferred language. Work address and work phone number. Enough personal information to make a person nervous if that person is into government conspiracies and takes things like *The Matrix* seriously. But what do we care about all that? Everyone has personal information. It's non-essential when you're checking out a book.

One field of information does, however, pop up on the screen that can instantly fill us with a vague sense of horror and dread. Above the patron's name, there may be a "notes" field that means something special has been added—something personal. The note may be something like this:

PATRON LEFT BIRTH CERTIFICATE IN COPIER. IN BACK ROOM AT NORTHWEST BRANCH.

Or:

PATRON HAS BEEN WARNED SEVERAL TIMES NOT TO RETURN AUDIOVISUAL ITEMS IN BOOKDROP. CDS ARE BEING DAMAGED. NO MORE FINES WILL BE WAIVED.

Or:

DO NOT CHARGE THIS PATRON FOR REQUESTS. SHUT-IN.

The notes field appears on the computer screen, the patron can peer over the counter and read the message, and it's self-explanatory. The harshest note in the notes field is the brief IN COLLECTION. There aren't many of these, because we haven't done this for the past five years or so, but if you're in collection you owe the city hundreds, and perhaps thousands, of dollars. If you're in collection, no, you can't check out a book. You can come in, look around, browse through the best sellers, but you can't walk out the door with a book. You can't even offer to write one of your bad checks. You're officially locked out of the system, and to get back in you have to appear at the city treasurer's office, head hung low, and maybe you should bring a lawyer with you.

The most dreaded message in the notes field, however, is this: MMM. There is no official definition of this code. It means: Guard your privates. Pat your wallet to make sure it's still there. Take a deep breath. This patron is going to be a real prick.

It's a good thing this brief code exists. If you're dealing with a serially abusive and potentially violent patron, he or she doesn't need to see the message THIS PATRON IS A REAL PRICK. It might make them prickier or give them legal recourse. MMM is insider stuff. If the patron gets suspicious and asks for an explanation, you can give him your much-honed bewildered look, shrug your shoulders, and there's a good chance he'll buy it.

My first MMM was an older woman checking out a book on how to gauge your emotional maturity and intelligence. It was one of my first evenings in the library where I was in charge, and there was no one to whom I could foist her off if the need arose. Terri had come in three hours early to pull all the books that were on the high school and junior high reading lists and put them in a single, conspicuous book trough near the front of the library, so she left a few hours early, and Juanita had skipped out to attend some special meeting of the City Council as a representative of the library. I was it.

The woman picked up the book she was thinking of checking out and asked me if I had read it. No, I said. There are many books in the library I have never read, heard of, or even touched. It seems like a commonsense notion. She moved back a step as if I had thrown a bucket of cold water at her. You haven't read the book? she replied. Then how can you tell me about it?

I told her I could look in the bibliographic record for the book in the computer and tell her all about it, or I could print out a review from Amazon.com, but that there were many books in the library I hadn't read.

She flinched again. You don't even read books? What kind of idiot are you? They should hire someone who reads—not you!

The abuse was so casual and unprovoked it felt like walking briskly into a closed door. She was the Muhammad Ali of vitriol.

Within forty seconds I had backed into the ropes, dazed, and was begging her to stop. Patrons with a flair for abuse have a natural edge; they're the public and therefore get to deal the cards. If as a public servant I choose to return the abuse, there's a justification for termination of employment. "You called her a what? Really? Oh dear. Please wait out in the hallway for a few moments while we make our deliberations." After she finally left, I noticed her notes field for the first time: MMM.

And then there is Mr. Jackson. Mr. Jackson is an angry man of about fifty-five. He wields a cane. When he checks out material at the main branch, he demands that the receipt be tucked in the second book down from the top. The receipt should be showing only a half inch or less. He can become abusive if the checkout person slips up and just puts the receipt on top of the books, or if the person behind the checkout desk takes the receipt and puts it too far inside one of the books. Ideally, it should be one-fourth of an inch out. Not too showy, not too hidden. The material he checks out should be alphabetized by the checkout person, A at the top, Z at the bottom.

At this point, you think I am lying to you just to make this a good story—that no one is that anal retentive, that no organization would let such a thing continue, or that I am purposely painting in broad, comic strokes to make a point. I am not.

Here's how I met the man.

I am working at the circulation desk at the main branch of the library, as I am required to do once every two weeks. It's late in the day, and he puts his books on the counter, then throws his library card on the counter in front of me. In the world of poker, throwing your library card at the checkout person is a tell. You do not have to look at the notes field and see MMM to figure it out. Throwing a library card, or a credit card, or a chilled martini at a person is a nonsubtle way of telling the person on the other side of the counter that you intend to eat their lunch. Not all of it, of course. Just a few, large bites.

I do not notice the notes field and the MMM anyway. It has

been a busy day. My back is tired from standing at the circulation desk that has been built to accommodate someone four feet tall, and I don't care that this angry man in front of me wants to be known as the sultan of swat. He and I both are pathetic little figures in life, he in his way, me in mine, and when he demands that I put the receipt into the second book from the top, I pick up the receipt and hand it to him, thinking: go wild.

And he does.

"Do it now," he says, when the transaction is over and I am ready to get on to the next person in line. "And put them in a bag!" He says this like it is the trump card of all trump cards, smiling, and I go underneath the counter and pull out a small, recycled plastic bag we keep for occasions just like this. I still don't get it. Finally, it dawns on me. He has been fucking with me for three minutes and I didn't get it. I thought he was being your average prick. Now I realize I have been wrong.

"Here's a bag," I say, and leave it on the counter. Then I walk back to the circulation desk. We're a library. We give away books. We lend out movies. We have free Internet access. But we have no procedures about stacking and alphabetizing checked-out material and automatically placing them in plastic bags. For that matter, we have plastic bags only because a local retailer gave us a few boxes of them during the last big rainstorm. It is a kindness, not a rigidly maintained internal procedure. So I ignore him.

He continues to shout, "Put my books into a goddamn bag! Now!"

I know I could be a better human being, but I am an old dog content with my many shortcomings. I do not automatically try to cheer up small children because they are pouting, nor do I pander to adults because they are petulant and acting like small children.

Here's the good part, not so much for him but for me. When people try to burn a civil servant to the ground by cursing and swearing, they paint themselves into a corner. I cannot reply in kind. I cannot say: Put the books in your own goddamn bag, fuckstick! Replies of this kind are grounds for dismissal. They can curse at you and you cannot curse back. All I could do was enrage him more, which I did.

"Sir," I told him, "this transaction is over." And I walk back to the next patron in line. I do this because it is the decent, Christian thing to do—to turn the other cheek—and I know if there is any chance of inducing an aneurysm in the old fool, this is it. I think he is somehow secretly happy that someone has finally decided to battle with him.

"Hey," he says. " Hey! You hear me? Damn it, put this shit in a goddamn bag!"

My anger rises to his taunt, like a big, fat, stupid trout on an insect-laden river in an early Hemingway novel. So I do what any civil servant does when attacked. I act officious.

"Sir, this transaction is over. You'll have to leave."

He begins to fairly dance in outrage. This is how he has been treated his whole life—shunted from one unsatisfying scene to the next. He wants resolution. He wants action! And I am the only lamb chop on the table. Then I say, "If you do not leave, I'll have to call security."

There are, at the main branch, now and again, from time to time, security guards. I do not know if this is one of those times. It is a semi-bluff and I am hoping one of the next few cards to be turned over is an ace. I push a button underneath the counter that will either call a security guard or buzz urgently in an empty room.

He says, "I'm going to come around there and take care of you! Take care of you right now!" Now, this is a threat. And a part of me thinks what an interesting story this will be some day. I am hoping that there will be a naturally occurring happy ending and not a contrived one where I am wheeled out of the library and into an emergency room with a broken face, just happy to be alive. As he makes his move to come around the counter, the security guard actually arrives, recognizes him, turns to me, and says something like, Oh! This guy! He's always giving someone a hard time.

Two more librarians show up, not so much to intercede but to witness the bloodshed and be included in the police report.

The man leans over the counter and hisses, "Next time I come here, I'm going to take care of you!"

I make many fans by replying, "I have time now. Take care of me now. Let's go." I know now that it was wrong of me to respond in this way, getting emotionally involved with an angry, perhaps unbalanced customer. It was a mistake, and I knew there was a good chance I'd have to sit in a room by myself and watch a forty-minute videotape on the folly of throwing down with an abusive patron. Peter Graves would narrate, and by his no-nonsense tone you'd know he would never do such a dumb-ass thing. I'd watch the story of a hardworking civil servant as he lost everything for one stupid, regrettable moment. He'd forfeit his job, then his house. His wife would cry and cry and shake her head, and her hair would be stringy and unconditioned to show graphically how disappointed she was. His kids wouldn't know exactly what happened, but they'd know that their dad had fucked up. They would figure that out just listening to Peter Graves's voice-over.

At the time, though, I thought it was win-win for me. I am telling the guy to go pound salt. The absolutely worst thing that could happen would be him eventually tap-dancing on my skull, and when that happens I will sue the city for putting me into a dangerous situation. I'll never have to work again. They'll send the checks straight to my house and I'll spend hours every day sweeping the beach for change with a new state-of-the-art metal detector and drinking the most complicated cups of coffee Starbucks has to offer.

But he is hustled outside and I am hustled to another room to cool off. No one gets to take care of anybody. I have so much adrenaline shooting through my body that my hands are shaking and my teeth are chattering. By the time I have calmed down and my body stops shaking, cooler heads within the library have collaborated to write a nicely paced first draft of the incident report, and all I have to do is initial it.

The security guard comes into the back room and tells me that Mr. Jackson is always yelling at someone, always threatening to sue, always threatening to go to the city manager. One of the reference librarians tells me he buzzes for security as soon as he sees the man. Three of the afternoon pages warmly congratulate me for threatening to take him outside and kick his ass, which is not exactly what happened, but it is good press. I don't even think of correcting them. It seems he has given everyone in the library a hard time.

I go to a computer screen later in the day and bring up his name. In the notes field: MMM. I add a second notes field and add it again: MMM. An additional flag is put on his notes field by library administration. The next time he comes in to check out material, he will have to have a brief sit-down with someone from administration and someone from the police department. They will touch all the bases as to what we expect from him as far as his behavior goes. The note stays on his screen for several years, but the sit-down never materializes. Mr. Jackson never comes back.

One of the female senior librarians who has been at the main library for years and years comes up to me later that day and tells me her stories about Mr. Jackson. He has been doing this for a long time. Looking at the computer screen, she admits that she put the first MMM note on his record years ago. Librarians have been using the code for a while.

She doesn't know what it means either, although she thinks it may mean "Makes Me Mad."

Or it might not.

Librarians are not good at getting mad. We're trained not to.

Chapter Nineteen
The Hair on the Back of Your Neck

THERE ARE NOT MANY PATRONS like the cane-wielding Mr. Jackson, but it was at least a happy thing that he announced his attitude and intentions while he was still in the library. More often, they are quiet, not outstanding, almost invisible, and leave mayhem in their wake that is only discovered long after they leave the library. These are the ones we're *really* concerned about.

The first time this happened was during the school year, late in the semester, maybe seven years ago, and I was standing in Adult Fiction, showing someone where we keep the way too many volumes of Danielle Steel. There was a normal thrum of activity, nothing unusual, nothing odd, and a man walked by me in a baseball cap, T-shirt, and baggy shorts. For two seconds, I thought, "You should keep your eye on this one." Then I looked at him more closely and wondered what the hell I was thinking. He was clean, had a recent haircut, wasn't talking to himself, didn't seem angry, and was carrying two books in his hands. He wasn't tentative, didn't seem to be looking for anyone, and seemed just like a thirty-five-year-old man looking for a place to sit, perhaps wondering why there weren't any. I forgot about him, turned back to the Danielle Steel woman, and listened to her extol Danielle Steel for about thirty seconds before I excused myself and began to drift back to the reference desk area.

For about two hours every weekday afternoon the place is packed, every seat is taken, there is a line at the reference desk, the homework helpers are overwhelmed, the pages are continually busy at the checkout desk, and the phone rings every three to four minutes, mostly reference questions regarding science projects, book reports, and that night's homework.

At 5:30 the same afternoon, Juanita brought a young girl into her office and closed the door. The girl was a fifth grader, a regular. She had a pink backpack with cartoon dogs on the back. Her face was wet and puffy from crying.

The girl had been sitting by herself, getting ready to do her homework, and a man came up to her and exposed himself. It was a planned thing. Then he walked away. She sat frozen in her seat, terrified, for a half hour until she was sure he was gone. Then she began to breathe again, found a librarian, and reported it. She described the man, and he was the guy I had noticed for two seconds and forgot about, same baseball cap, T-shirt, and baggy shorts. He was, of course, no longer in the library.

On a Saturday a few years later, an enormous three-hundred-pound plus man with a wild beard and a filthy serape came into the library, and there was the same feeling. Vague dread. Just the smallest whisper in the head, "Watch him! Do not take your eyes off him!" He sat at a desk right in front of the reference desk for the better part of an afternoon, quietly enraged, and spent the whole time writing the longest and angriest of letters on a lined yellow tablet. Just before closing, he asked for an envelope to mail his letter, and we gave him a large manila envelope. He stuffed his letter inside. Then he sealed it shut and "mailed" it by stuffing it inside the dictionary stand, which kind of looks like a mailbox if you're on any number of psychotropic drugs.

When the library was closed, we retrieved the letter, opened the envelope, and looked at the contents. It was fourteen pages of:

ℓℓℓℓ ℓℓℓ ℓℓℓℓℓℓℓ ℓℓℓℓ ℓℓℓℓ ℓℓℓ

This was not angry, illegible handwriting; it was just one long doodle, broken up into words. Fourteen pages of angry nothing. The letter so unnerved us that we stayed for a half hour past closing writing up an incident report and kept the letter in the back room for a few years in case he came back, wondering why his damn letter had never been delivered.

A few years ago, a community lead officer came into the library during the dead hours between one to three o'clock. Ostensibly, he came because we were in the middle of banning Angelica Williams/ Ramsay/Dashell/Marquez and her boys from the branch. Anyway, the officer touched on the snap judgment thing, those times when for no reason at all a person walks into the library and the hair on the back of your neck stands up. He thought it was a good thing to heed, and a mistake to dismiss. He even recommended a book we already had on our shelves, *Blink* by Malcolm Gladwell, that explored the wisdom of acting on these two-second intuitive impulses. He was kind of surprised we hadn't already read it, but he didn't try to rub it in.

During the first few weeks of the school year this year Keiko, the afternoon page, came up to me and pointed to a man. "Watch this one," she said. She did not give a reason. Another one of the afternoon pages approached me at the reference desk. "The guy at the middle table," she said. "He's sitting with children and he shouldn't be." Terri noticed him next. She couldn't put a finger on it but thought there was something creepy about him. A man in his twenties chatting up fifth graders.

Terri went over to the table and said hi to the girls doing their homework there. The middle-school girls love Terri. She listens to them and laughs at their jokes and is honestly moved by their simple gestures. They make her bracelets and necklaces and she wears them the rest of the day or until they fall apart and fall off on their own.

One of them grabbed Terri's wrist and whispered in her ear, "Don't leave!"

We called the police and they came almost immediately. They asked to speak to the man outside and he was stunned. Outraged. What did they think he was doing? What kind of place was this, what kind of people were we to call the police because you made small talk with children? What kind of a world were we living in? What did they think he was, a pervert? Was he under arrest?

Inside, Terri's young friend approached her and thanked her for not leaving the table. The man had come up and started talking like he had known them for years. He wanted to know how old they were, what they liked to do, what kind of sports they were involved in, what sorts of animals they liked. They answered him because he was an adult and it would have been rude not to, but something about him made them feel sick. Terri told them if he came back inside, they could all sit in the back room until he left. They asked if they could call their parents to pick them up, and Terri called their parents.

The same man came in again the next afternoon, shortly before school got out. He came up to the reference desk and wanted to clear the air. He was extremely agitated.

"Someone called the police on me yesterday," he said.

"Yes," I answered.

"Who was it? I want to talk to that person."

I was that person but I didn't care what he wanted, so I lied. "I don't know who called the police, but perhaps I can help you."

"Well, why were the police called?"

I said, "Did the police explain themselves?"

He shook his head in disgust. "I don't know what you people think I did. I just talked to some of the kids. It was all innocent stuff. If they said anything else, they're lying to you. Kids lie a lot."

"Oh," I said.

"I could sue the city for something like that."

"Yes."

"I just like to talk to people, that's all."

"Oh."

"I'll talk to whoever the hell I want to."

"Yes," I said. "I think the library feels that same way about calling the police when we think it's necessary."

"What if I talk to them outside?"

"I don't know what you mean."

"What if I just talk to them on the sidewalk? That's not a crime, is it?"

I resented being in this conversation. I wanted to say something rude, just to let him know that we were on to him, but I didn't. I had a feeling there was a forty-minute video called "Being a Wise-Ass Is Never Good" that had my name on it.

"The police have urged library personnel to contact them whenever we feel it's appropriate."

"Why? Just tell me what I'm doing that's so wrong."

"The police should be able to help you with that, too."

On the way out, he turned and spat out: "You people think I'm some kind of pervert, don't you?"

"Oh," I said.

It was the tail end of a very interesting school year.

Chapter Twenty
The Last Day of School

THE SCHOOL YEAR HAD BEEN pretty successful. Terri started up her teen book group and it was a moderate but unmistakable success, the academic decathlon team camped out in the farthest, quietest corner of the juvenile section every Tuesday, Wednesday, and Thursday until we closed and had to kick them out, the high school tutors came every day they were supposed to, and at the time they were supposed to whoever was pissing and crapping all over the walls of the men's restroom suddenly stopped, and we didn't have to call the police once.

Until the last day of the year.

Some years we call the police a lot—so much so that we feel the police treat us with a certain disdain. You call the police complaint number that is tacked up on the bulletin board in back and you just feel some police operator rolling her eyes when she hears that it's the library. Better send over a busload of the riot squad, the librarians have a bunch of fidgety kids who won't do their homework and are probably giggling into their fists. But calling the police is what we're supposed to do in certain circumstances, so we call. Depending on how busy they are, they may arrive in five minutes, several hours, or not at all. They do not like to feel they are coming just to admonish small children who have said naughty words in an outside voice.

We didn't predict trouble on the last day of school. It's too late for drama. The whole damn thing is almost over. The elementary-school kids come into the library with a year's worth of worksheets, reports, and crayoned projects. The middle-school kids are exhausted. Their teachers have had to turn in the textbooks a week earlier, and the teachers have been playing it by ear ever since, like comedians who have run out of material and discover they have six minutes left to fill. Some teachers give tests that fill the time, and these tests are never graded, looked at, or returned. Others pop in a video that has some tenuous educational value, or throw wretched little parties, anything to make the clock move. The high school students simply disappear.

So it was curious when one of the middle-school girls came up to the reference desk and told us two girls were fighting in the parking lot. There's simply no motivation to do this kind of thing on the last day. We were in the denouement part of the school year, so we figured it was some kind of gag. But schoolkids know where the action is. It's a gift. From all over the library they dropped their rulers and protractors and stuffed backpacks and streamed outside to see the girls fight, so a few librarians streamed along with them.

Yes, there was a real fight. Two girls were rolling around on the asphalt parking lot, pulling hair, punching, scratching each other in the face, grabbing great handfuls of whatever they could reach and smacking it. Juanita needed only a brief look to know there was no way she was getting in the middle of *that*, and the way she said it made it sound like a good plan for the rest of us, too. Trying to break it up might have cost a tooth or a pair of pants. I went outside, yelled at them to break it up, they ignored me, and I went back inside. Now seemed like one of those times to call the police.

Terri noticed it first.

"Oh, shit," she said, and a few little kids standing around her gasped and snickered, looking around to see who else had heard the librarian swear. It's great to hear a librarian curse. It would make such a good story that night at the supper table when Mom or Dad had a mouthful of mashed potatoes.

Terri looked at me. "Those aren't girls." I noticed it then, too. They weren't school girl clothes, and they weren't wearing school girl shoes. Middle-school girls don't wear high heels and panty hose and they don't bash each other with expensive purses filled with wallets and credit cards and birth control pills. These were women—mothers. They had come to the library to pick up their children, and now they were rolling around in the parking lot like partially disemboweled hyenas, spitting blood, trying to choke the life out of each other.

We found out later it happened something like this:

Two of the eighth graders were best friends. They walked to school together, ate lunch together, and they called each other every night to see what they had missed that day, what the homework assignments were, and what they were going to wear to school the following day. Friends. The friendship somehow unraveled on the last day of school and their feelings were both hurt. There were a few tears.

When the moms pulled into the parking lot, they knew nothing of this inconsequential tragedy. The women knew each other and knew the girls. One noticed her daughter had been crying. The girl was questioned and she pointed to the other girl. Her mom figured it out. She stopped the other girl and asked for a full explanation. The other mom announced tersely that the two were no longer friends.

Then why did she make my daughter cry?

No one made your daughter cry. She's immature.

I want an explanation.

Get your hands off of my daughter!

I need an explanation right now!

I will remove your hands myself if you do not remove them!

Bitch!

And so on.

The women wrestled on the ground until the police showed up, and the presence of authority and the promise of pepper spray caused the women to fall apart, exhausted. It went well beyond broken lips, scraped knees, and ripped fingernails. They had black eyes and discolored throats, their clothes were ruined, and both had pulled out substantial chunks of luxurious hair, roots included. The daughters had both retreated back inside the library, and as things calmed down they began to sob. A failed friendship is one thing to deal with—watching your mother being choked out in the parking lot of a public library with your best friend's mother on top of her is quite another. Both mothers were willing and eager to press charges, and they were taken away on two stretchers and two ambulances to be examined and X-rayed and bandaged, and also to be photographed and fingerprinted and booked.

The two ex-friends lived next door to each other. They walked home but not together.

On the following Monday, one of the women came in with her husband and a third person who was presumably her lawyer. The woman wore her hair in a way that tried to hide the missing chunks. She wore a neck brace. Wherever you saw skin, there were black-and-blue marks. She would be a beautiful woman again, but it was going to take a little time. Her husband was angry and obnoxious. Who had seen the other woman attack his wife? Who? Was it you? Talk to me!

The person who was presumably the lawyer was quietly gregarious and efficient, speaking to everyone for a few seconds and leaving everyone his card.

An hour or so later, the second couple came in with their lawyer. The tableau was the same: ruined wife, angry husband, and unctuous mouthpiece. It was shaping up as quite a battle and would have made a fine summer replacement series on some struggling television network.

But none of us knew who threw the first punch, who knocked the first hand aside. The middle schoolers didn't know either, but they couldn't wait for school to begin again in the fall so they could ask the two girls hundreds of questions. They never got the chance. Both families sold their homes and moved back to Korea, effectively washing their hands of the whole fiasco. I hope they moved to different towns.

Chapter Twenty-one
The Summer Crew

IT IS DOWNRIGHT HOT OUTSIDE, and the kids don't have to be kicked out of the library for bad behavior—it's too much fun to be outside, screaming, running, riding their bikes, being outrageous on skateboards. There is a piquancy, something they will know one day as nostalgia, for the school year has come to an end. As always, there will be different faces next year, friends will have moved away, abruptly and without warning. It is a transient crowd. They move away with borrowed basketballs, iPods, yearbooks, and library material by the ton. Threaten them with legal action by mail and the post office returns the letters. They're no longer there. They've been swallowed by the earth—moved to another part of the city, another city, another state, sometimes another country altogether.

Then it is July. Finally, it is summer. The sidewalk is warm by nine a.m., and it is a bright balmy world of sun, a few clouds, a twilight breeze that pushes the heat out of the bedroom, and no one is under the illusion that there are rain clouds on the horizon. Los Angeles is, after all, a desert. Forget to water your lawn a few days in a row and the grass wilts and turns crunchy, and it is like walking on a thin layer of cornflakes. It is not a pleasant sensation. My raised bed garden in the backyard is beginning to face a similar stress. Uneven watering pro-duces defective vegetables—cucumbers that are heavy with moisture on one end, gaunt, yellow, and shriveled at the other, eggplants that lean, dehydrated, the whole plant dipping to the ground to ease the burden of the heavy fruit.

I water the garden in the early morning before I go to the library, when it is cool and there is a good chance I will be bitten by a mosquito and contract the West Nile River virus. I do not care. The newspaper articles I read imply that we will all get it eventually. Perhaps it is better to get infected while there are still lots of healthy people left to take care of me. I know what I'm talking about here. I've read Dafoe's *Journal of the Plague Year*.

The library is putting the final touches on the Summer Reading Program, as it does every summer. People who have not been in the library for nine months now stream back in with their children. When school is in session, the library is a holding facility for recalcitrant youth. But in the summer the schools are mostly empty, and the library as detention facility is deserted. The schoolkids do not as a rule come back in the summer. Even if they lay on sofas all summer and stare at the ceiling, sick of the television, bored to tears by their dated, archaic collection of expensive computer games, they never consider the library an option.

We will see these children again in the fall, their faces filled out and more defined, inches taller, their voices deeper, but with the same wild, cursed hopelessness in their eyes as they stumble into the library to burn away more precious hours of their youth before their own adulthood rescues them. Oh no, they will not come back to visit. It is a whole different crew in the summer.

The summer crew is mostly preschoolers and their mothers and first-generation Americans trying to get a handle on the language. The library is nearby. It is free. The young children believe that a trip to the library is an adventure. They are there, standing in the shade under the trees in front of the library, waiting in front of the locked doors at 10 a.m., and they come in regularly throughout the day, thinning out at nap time and then coming on strong again around 3 to 6 p.m.

Last year's summer reading club revolved around the wild west. Cacti, horses, whirlwinds, Gila monsters. Terri and another one of the branch librarians went out and rented a half dozen bales of hay to add to the ambience in the library. Terri also purchased handkerchiefs so we could tie them around our necks and look—I guess—like cowboy librarians. She stayed away from the red ones and the blue ones, because we didn't want to be mistaken for L.A. gang members, especially *by* L.A. gang members. Lillian the senior librarian even obtained a number of tiny red cowboy hats that she believed would be a perfect accoutrement to the ensemble, but no one would touch them. Past a certain age, tiny red cowboy hats only add to the dipshit quotient. They wound up gathering dust in the back room, until Terri's next wave of OCD compelled her to put them all into a packing box that she labeled "cowboy hats."

The summer reading club is the tradition of traditions in the public library, and if you do a Web search on the term, you will find remarkably similar programs in Kennebunkport, Memphis, Detroit, and Key West. The summer reading club is a mechanism that pulls in a whole new group of kids who have otherwise not entered the library in the past nine months. It is a curious business. The day-to-day regulars during the school year are conspicuously absent during the summer, and the kids who establish themselves in the library during the summer dry up and blow away once school is in session. Oh, the children's librarians would like to know why it is thus, but it is a mystery.

One year, a coven of children's librarians even fashioned the equivalent of exit interviews, which they gave to the departing families of summer readers in August. But they were children's librarians, not demographers, so the questions were vaguely upbeat, slightly biased, ever so wrongheaded, and they didn't have a clue as to how to decipher their own results. The questionnaires were stored in a similar packing box at the main library.

The summer reading club is a tradition that has been around a long time and changed little. There is a theme. One year it is all about reptiles. Billy the boa constrictor says: Wrap yourself around a good read. Ricky the rattlesnake shakes his tail for a hot book. The next year it is all about a penguin in a trench coat who seems to be a private eye — Want a hot tip, kids? The library is a coo-o-o-l place to find all sorts of interesting books.

Every year there is a new batch of talking animals that want to sell you on the library. Vinnie the velociraptor can't wait to dig his claws into a good book. Danny the dinosaur. Whatever. The theory — and I believe it — is that it's not necessary to change the formula too much, because within a year or two there's a whole new audience walking in the front door. By the time you're fourteen or fifteen, Minnie the mastodon is not going to get you into the library. At this point, you're either a reader or you're not. If you are a reader, you'll walk in, see the posters for the summer reading club for Bobo the black bear, cringe nostalgically, and not break stride.

It's also a money thing. The city wants to back its fire department, its 911 operators, and its police force, they want to be able to cut down dead trees and repair pot holes in the streets, and throwing any kind of money into a publicity campaign to get kids into the library almost seems wasteful.

This year, the theme for the summer reading club is superheroes. There is a T-shirt available that shows a smiling, muscled superhero in green and yellow tights (a guy) throwing some kind of energy ball at an unseen foe. It is not Green Lantern, and it is not Superman, Batman, Wolverine, Captain America, Magneto, Flash, Spider-Man, the Hulk, Silver Surfer, not even Warrior Nun Arella. It's nobody. The licensing fees would have killed us. It would have been enough to gobble up the salary for a full-time paramedic or a patrol dispatcher, and that would have been insane. A generic superhero will have to save us.

So you walk into the library, there's a central, zany theme that may or may not include talking animals or people in brightly colored spandex, you sign up, you join the summer reading club, and there are little perks throughout the summer to keep you interested. At the end of the program, in the beginning of August, there's the equivalent of a puppet show, after which time any fool knows that it's over.

You read books. You hit certain levels. You hit certain achievement levels and your parents get to feel like they're doing a pretty goddamn good job. The library tries to stay away from the idea of passing and failing, because a whiff of failure might keep a young person away from the library for the rest of his life. Really, what fourth grader needs the first acrid taste of bitter grapes doled out to him by the public library in the middle of summer?

Oh no.

Everyone passes.

If you finish one book in eight weeks and you're proud of yourself, we're proud of you too. One book it is. If you're of a certain compulsive bent and read thirty-five Nancy Drew mysteries over the summer, we're prepared to be impressed. Reading is a good thing.

But when the library decides to foster a bit of competition, it always gets ugly. In one of my first years, each person entered in the Summer Reading Program got a small, brightly colored paper boat, and the little paper boat sailed around the cinder-block walls of the library in a giant happy regatta. Each book that was read took the small boat another six inches. At first, a few of the more prolific readers put some distance between themselves and the pack, but it didn't last long.

Some kids began to lie about the number of books they read, and other kids who were shy about lying weren't shy about pulling their own boat off the wall and throwing it into the lead. After the first three weeks, only a few dozen kids stayed becalmed near the starting line. A few of the families had moved. And the others just didn't have the kind of peer-inspired bloodlust—homeschoolers, probably—and so they wandered about the harbor, losers with broken rudders or flooded engines, waiting for the coast guard to tow them back into the harbor. We cheered them up and told them it didn't matter, it wasn't really a race, but we might as well have festooned their little boats with paper flames, cotton balls of smoke, and the suggestion of a tiny oil slick.

Kids are insane. They want to compete, but reading is a non-competitive thing. As soon as there is a measure to gauge difference, their tails are wagging, they are gnawing at their cages, and they are aching to compete with and destroy the other children.

One year, we tried a different tactic. Read five books and win a prize. After five books, you're shooting blanks. Read a thousand more and we couldn't care less. You're only going to get recognition for the first five. And the prize? Might be a pencil. Might be a paperback book. Might be a coupon for a free pizza at a local chain. There were, of course, a lot more pencils than there were pizza coupons, and the kids began to reenter just to get another shot at the free pizza. It was pretty much the end of things when one teary-eyed girl won another pencil and pleaded with Terri for one more shot at the golden ticket. She wanted a recount, special consideration, accommodation, dispensation, anything. Anything but another goddamn pencil.

Terri was moved by the girl's tears and told her to put her hand in the plastic jar and pull out another ticket. She won another pencil. And so she kept on drawing until she hit the pizza certificate. It was all downhill after that.

The worst year of the summer reading club—the most humiliating, and the one we'd all most like to forget—was the year some organization kicked in a grand prize of airfare and tickets for two to a space camp in Houston, Texas. One winner from all the libraries would be able to take his or her mom or dad or a best friend and attend a crazy, high-tech space camp in Houston for seven days. It was an extraordinary prize. Second prize might have been a set of steak knives. And third prize, as always, pencils. The competition started as a well-intentioned thing. Read a book of a hundred pages or more and get a ticket—a chance, a lottery ticket—on winning the grand prize. We thought it would fire the kids up to read more and thus win more tickets.

By the second day of the promotion, a few kids had already figured it out. A little girl about twelve or thirteen came up to the reference desk with a stack of fifteen books and asked very politely for her fifteen tickets.

Had she read them all?

Why, yes, yes, she had.

Overnight?

Yes.

Since yesterday.

Yes.

Not over the past year—since yesterday.

Yes.

And that was it; that was the dilemma in a nutshell. In one day, a girl declared that she had read approximately 1,600 pages. Not counting sleep, dinner and going to the bathroom, she had been banging through about two pages a minute for the past twenty-four hours. Do you shrug your shoulders and admit you've been had, or do you slam your fist on the table, stare the little girl in the eye, and call her a little bald-faced, rat bastard liar?

On the other hand, this *is* the public library. You'd have to go to Las Vegas or parts of Tibet for more freakish behavior. Maybe she had read fifteen books overnight. Bizarre, yes. Sick, unhealthy, wrongheaded, and perverse, yes. But this is the public library. When you think about it, we're the ones encouraging this behavior. Sitting inside during the summer and reading books. The little girl heard our message and slid all her chips into the pot.

Terri, as the children's librarian, had to be the one to make the call. It was an ugly dilemma, and there was no diplomatic answer. But Terri thought it was the wrong move to get into the name-calling thing, so she suggested we start asking one or two pertinent questions about each book.

But this girl had been raised by goblins and elves and wizards and card sharks.

I held up a Judy Blume book and asked her what the book was about.

She pointed to an illustration of a girl on the cover and said, "Her."

"What about her?" I asked.

"It's about the adventures she has."

"What kind of adventures?"

"All kinds."

"Like what?"

"She gets into trouble."

"Really? That doesn't sound good. What kind?"

"With her parents."

The illustration on the cover showed a freckle-faced girl holding a skateboard, a large dog that seemed to be cheering her on, and two parents, the mom discombobulated like she might explode, body parts rupturing and flying across the living room, and dad, his arms folded, gravely concerned, his brain beginning to smolder like a terry-cloth towel draped across a toaster.

I'm sure I could have broken her if I had the proper funding and a lot more time, but I didn't have either. I hadn't read the book. She could have told me it was all about a strung-out little girl who steals her parents' credit cards, travels to New York with a telepathic monkey, dyes her hair blonde, makes a lot of money on a network game show, and then goes blind. I would have agreed and said: Oh god, what a sad book. What did I know? For all I knew, she had read the book and was simply doing a miserable job of talking about it.

I didn't think so, but anything was possible. Maybe my interrogation technique, honed from too many *Law and Order* episodes, was making her shut down. If I didn't back off, she'd lawyer up and the library would be screwed. I was plagued with doubt for the better part of twenty-four hours when she came back into the library again with another fifteen books. At this rate, by the end of the summer reading club, she'd have stuffed the ballot box with more than four hundred entries.

But how much was I supposed to care?

What did anyone care? The library was tickled that the books were checked out, Terri's boss was pleased that our juvenile statistics were so much improved, the little girl's parents were happy that she was so obviously fitting in with the whole "ruin your summer reading" thing, and the girl was making bank.

By the end of the summer she had indeed made bank. Other kids won erasers, free orders of french fries, little black monsters that were said to glow in the dark, and sad kaleidoscopes so painfully cheap that they did nothing. You held them to the light and peered through an opening and rotated the thing, looking at nothing, until finally, in despair and frustration, you smacked the goddamn thing with an office stapler to break it into pieces just to see what the hell was going on inside. It was perfect for a six-year-old to win as a free prize in the middle of summer.

Of course the little girl won the main prize. They drew her name, and we all went numb, knowing that we had helped to birth this great miscarriage of justice, that we had done nothing to stop it, and that we had better shut up about it and do our bitching in private.

The theme the following year was aliens and flying saucers. "Take me to your reader!" "These books are out of this world!" No one solicited donations for prizes, and everyone who entered the summer reading club that year wound up with a ball-tip pen or a pencil that said SUMMER READING PROGRAM. Some of the pencils glowed in the dark, but that might have been due to a glitch in the manufacturing process. Only a few of the parents complained and told us we were on a slippery slope to a real crap summer reading club, but we figured the complainers were this year's ringers, ready to knock the ball out of the park.

Some kids who were awarded the pens and pencils actually lit up and were excited that they were getting something for free for doing something as pleasurable as reading a book. To a few librarians, this planted a seed that better prizes the following year might even give the kids more impetus.

You know, to read.

Chapter Twenty-two
Love Stories

LOVE STORIES ARE SCARCE IN THE LIBRARY, and this might have something to do with the fact that we tell people to knock it off and take it outside, which is not a good way for a love story to begin. There are quite a few romantics punching the clock for the library, so in the abstract we are rooting for young lovers, but only in the abstract. We don't want urgent fumblings in the adult nonfiction stacks, unzipped jeans, or indiscreet wetness. The janitors will have to bring out their most powerful chemicals and an assortment of disinfectants, and the sharp zip of ammonia will give us all headaches.

The main branch of the library had the crown jewel of romantic stories, but it was so scandalous and seemingly D. H. Lawrence–inspired that they're playing it close to the vest and not talking about it much. Turns out one employee fell in love with another. And not just any employees.

Suneeta was born in Pakistan, raised in the United States. She is a quiet, demure, intelligent young woman who, if things had worked out differently, could have made a large fortune as an exotic dancer. She has long, jet-black hair, wavy, that falls almost to her waist. She has a face that could make a tropical flower bloom, and a figure that you could stare at all day long. Though that would be wrong. You would know that if you sat through the videotape.

When she first started working for the library, we more or less figured she would not last long. Give her a month or two and she'd wind up as a personal trainer for a wealthy CEO, a Hollywood agent, an executive assistant in a fast-growing software company, a high-end manufacturer's rep, or any one of a hundred professions where she would become immediately and wildly successful. But she did not. She was going for a master's degree in Library Science.

We also assumed that she would be whisked away by a man in a certain profession—a doctor, a lawyer, a microbiologist, an endocrinologist, a plastic surgeon—someone working in a rarefied profession that paid outrageous bucks. But she didn't bump into anesthesiologists and gastroenterologists in the library. While they were scrubbing up and leafing through a patient's intestines, Suneeta was in the basement of the library, learning the driest and dullest of library alchemy—technical processing.

Technical processing is what has to be done to every book that is pulled into the system. Cowboys do it and call it branding, but in the library it is much more complex, more arcane. Technical processing is eight hours a day sitting in an uncomfortable chair, staring at a computer screen that is all lines and fields of information, with almost no human contact. In our library system, we call the people who work in technical processing basement dwellers. Gollum was probably a civil servant in such a field. It's how he got the way he was.

Harold is the head of technical processing and is responsible for what is called the Bibliographic Record for every book in the library. When I first met Harold, his idea of big fun was ordering Thai noodles and a diet Pepsi and eating them at his desk with the radio turned on ever so quietly to a station where the music strained to be inoffensive.

One Friday afternoon at quitting time, well into the first year of her stay in technical processing, someone noticed that Harold was giving Suneeta a ride home. The first thought was that Suneeta had some kind of car trouble. But that wasn't it at all. They had fallen in love behind our backs, the sly dogs. They left the building together on

Friday night and returned together on Monday morning. They were happy and more than a little goofy. Suneeta would come to his desk and Harold would ignore the monitor in front of him and speak to her, making small jokes that she would laugh at. Once, while they were standing at the back door, Harold unself-consciously and warmly put a hand on her waist.

Librarians are a scurrilous but romantic group. We ignored them as much as was humanly possible, and their romance continued to blossom. Eventually, they had a large wedding. Many city employees attended, and their wedding presents were uniformly practical and well thought out. Today, several years later, they still sit in the basement and look at each other across a room of fluorescent lights and computer screens and smile quiet smiles, meant only for each other.

At the branch library, we have had our own slice of this romance business. Michael and Rebekah met each other in a free class given for disabled adults. How to make breakfast. How to use the transit system. How to use the pay phone. Making change. Writing a check. Asking for directions. Buying groceries. Using the crosswalk.

Michael is in his early thirties but could be mistaken for a high school student. He is enthusiastic about life in general, gregarious in front of people he regards as friends, and as handsome and unremarkable as the next person on the street. He lived with elderly parents when he was younger, and with their help, moved into a halfway house for several years, where he started to learn how to take care of himself. From there, he graduated into a kind of independent, subsidized housing, and within certain narrow parameters he is able to take care of himself.

Rebekah is about the same age, blonde, petite, and naïve and open in a way that could become dangerous. She seems to have no relatives and no friends outside of Michael. She cannot live independently. She also has some neurological problems that are sometimes more or less under control. When it is less, her gait is affected, her posture, and her speech. She needs a lot of help.

Michael began to help her, and coming from Michael, it seemed to make more sense. He took Rebekah into a drugstore and helped her pick out a shampoo and conditioner. He helped her fill out the paperwork at a video store so she could walk in and rent videos. He brought her into the library and they both filled out library card applications.

Rebekah made Michael want to be more independent than ever. They came into the library and checked out a few videos to celebrate Michael's landing a part-time job at a craft store. Michael asked Terri for help putting together a résumé. He wanted to be able to rent a larger place so Rebekah could move in with him. Terri was touched. She went home and retyped his résumé in Microsoft Word, cleaned it up, and printed out twenty copies on good paper. There wasn't much on the résumé, and she told him that she could print out more if the first batch wasn't enough.

Michael couldn't find full-time work, so he took any part-time job that was offered. Most of them were one-time stints, sympathy jobs, but he didn't know that. He figured this was how careers started out. Rebekah made him Campbell's soup and simple sandwiches cut on the diagonal—she learned to do that at a class on foods. There were no similar employment prospects for her.

They came into the library, ashen, and returned four videos that were twenty days overdue. A dollar a day. Eighty dollars. Terri went to the front, waived the fines, and reminded them to be more careful. It was easy for this kind of thing to happen. Everyone did it sooner or later. No big deal. They left with a huge burden taken off their shoulders. Michael was happy to have a girlfriend like Rebekah and a friend like Terri.

Michael took a job at a fast-food restaurant on the graveyard shift. By now, Rebekah and Michael were living together, and Rebekah waited up every night until 3 a.m., when Michael came in after walking home from work, often with free bags of cold burgers. This, he told us, was one of his many perks. But the buses stopped running at midnight.

Michael told Terri that one of the things he wanted to do

with the extra money he was going to make was take them all out to dinner—Terri, Michael, and Rebekah. And yes, Terri's husband, Curtis. Terri knew immediately that it was a half-assed idea, but it became more horrible the more she thought about it. Michael was a patron, not really a friend. She had befriended him, but she had nothing really to say to him. There was no way in the world he could afford to buy dinner for four people. The idea filled her with a palpable dread. Curtis said he would go to this dinner if so ordered, but he intended to drink his way through it.

Not that it mattered in the long run. Michael came in about a week later and told Terri that the job was over. The deep fryer scared him. When the buzzer went off and announced that the fries were ready to come out of the boiling oil, he couldn't do it. The buzzer rattled and distracted him, and the hot oil seemed menacing and alive. He learned how to punch a red button that would turn the buzzer off. But then the fries stayed in the boiling oil and began to smoke. There is little forgiveness on the graveyard shift in the fast-food world. They had to get rid of him.

But he had what Terri thought was an excellent idea. He took several books on crafts out of the library. All he had to do was figure out something that he and Rebekah could do at home—like paintings or something—and that would solve all their problems. They'd work on them all day long, like a real job, and sell them at craft fairs. Terri waived another $50 in overdue fines and wished them the very best of luck.

Two weeks later, Terri had a painted popsicle-stick house on her desk. Michael brought it in as a present, but Terri gave him $20. They looked like they hadn't been eating. Michael told her that he and Rebekah could make three of the houses a day, which worked out to around $400 a week if they worked weekends. And why not? As long as they were together. It wasn't as if they threw their money away on expensive fun. They went to the park and fed the pigeons and the ducks. They took the bus to the beach, and they watched free videos from the library. They were so close to having it all.

Michael took another job working in food services for a large company downtown. Forty hours a week. It lasted only three days, because Rebekah could not be by herself for such a long stretch. He couldn't stand to see her so scared and anxious, so he called the company's employment number and told them to mail him a check for whatever he had earned. What else could he do? Terri could only shake her head.

Every four to six weeks, Terri was paged to the front desk to talk to Michael and waive his substantial fines. Michael was always contrite and sorry, often reduced to frightened tears, but he said that Rebekah liked to watch the same movie over and over again. It deepened her understanding of what was going on in the movie. Terri had told him several times she could no longer subsidize their overdue fines but, when they came in again with the same story, she did. She saw no alternative to being their financial booty call. They were abusing the system, but it wasn't as if they were being willful or malicious. Terri figured the system was made to accommodate such individuals.

Eventually, Michael came in and said that he had to speak to Terri privately. He told her that a group of men in similar gray suits were following him around the city. They looked into his windows at night, followed him down the block to the store, and got off the bus when he got off the bus. He was afraid that they were laying the groundwork for breaking into his apartment when he wasn't there and scaring Rebekah, maybe even raping her. Terri found it hard to respond in a meaningful way. Waiving fines was suddenly not nearly enough.

A week later, Michael and Rebekah came into the library to say good-bye to everyone. Michael had found a job through the Internet, and they were going to take a bus to Minnesota. They were done with Los Angeles and done with California. They were going to use Michael's secret stash of money to get them there. Rebekah had color pictures of Minnesota in a manila envelope. Michael could have moved back into subsidized housing, but Rebekah would not have been permitted to stay there, so that was out. It would have been too big of a step backward. Rebekah, too, could have gone back, but it frightened her now to be without Michael. Being together was the main thing, no matter what.

They wanted to hug everyone. Terri hugged them both for the rest of us and then Michael and Rebekah held each other's hands and said good-bye.

After they left, Terri sat in the back room, in tears. Before they'd left, Michael had come over to her, gave her a final hug, and whispered, "We're not really going to Minnesota!" He had a smile like the sweetest, saddest three-year-old in the world. And then they waved, and opened the door, and were gone. Hand in hand, walking down the street. Toward something that Rebekah thought was Minnesota but Michael knew was something else.

Chapter Twenty-three
Vacation Time

VACATIONS ARE A TRICKY THING in the library. There is never a good time to take one. Summer is absolutely out because of the Summer Reading Program. No one gets a pass during the Summer Reading Program. You would have to disguise it as an out-of-town funeral for a loved one, and let the chips fall where they may if you came back with a deep tan or pictures of yourself holding an eight-pound trout. The school year is also out, because the library is flooded after school with kids who have nowhere else to go. The days around Christmas are tough because someone else at your library has already requested this time off, perhaps as long as a year ago, and if someone else is off you can't go. The resources are spread too thin.

The library is traditionally short-staffed. When the after-school kids pour in, there may be 120 of them and at most five of us, pretending to be in charge. On a calmer Saturday, there may be only three of us—a page stranded behind checkout, a librarian anchored behind the reference desk, and the third person answering phones, floating, doing shelf checks, and relieving the other two for pee breaks.

On occasion, it dips down to two people, and that is never good. One page sits behind the checkout desk and the other person does whatever else is needed. When there are only two people working at the library, even a small, neighborhood library like mine, the normal flow of work grinds to a stop. There is no way to attend to things—you have to concentrate on attending to people and answering the phone. Someone drops off a large donation outside the back of the library— what do you do? Leave it. Piles of books need to be discharged? Leave it. Just leave it. The books will not feel ignored, the patrons will. An ignored patron can turn salty.

When the employee level dips to one—one person in a library with a key to the front door, ready to open the door to business—library administration shakes its head and says: No. Call another library and get someone else over there. Call a few of the other branches and see if they can shake loose a page or an assistant librarian to drive over. But you can't open with one employee. You'd be overwhelmed in the first ten minutes.

Understaffing the library makes good sense. With an ever di- minishing amount of money to be spent on civil servants, would you rather have an extra librarian, an extra 911 operator, or an extra fire- man? Everyone knows the answer to that one.

Administration tenses up when you ask for a week's vacation, and at least half of the time you'll be asked to reschedule. Whenever it is, it's not a good time. Ideally, they send out vacation request forms in January, so you can request the time off up to a year in advance, and even here they urge you to pencil in a second and a third choice— just, you know, in case.

After six or seven years the vacation hours build up. You have a vacation hour maximum allowed by the city, and you begin bumping into that. The danger is that once you go over the maximum, you ac- crue nothing. No more vacation hours for you. So as a defensive thing, every few years you can cash out. Take a check instead of a vacation. I have done this, and it feels vaguely dirty, as if you have just auctioned off a newborn child in exchange for a really nice sailboat or a bar of silver. But what else is there? You constantly accrue, few times are good, and the hours begin to bump into each other, like logs on a rain-swollen river. Soon there is a logjam, and things get worse from there.

One year, enough was enough, and I decided to take the family to Hawaii. The places in Hawaii are booked up for months, years in advance, and so I wrote up a vacation request four months earlier than is requested. There is this house in Kauai, there are pictures on the Internet, it is next to a river, next to Hanalei Bay, and I knew it would not last long. The library bent policy and granted me the time off.

My oldest daughter, Andrea, did not like Kauai. There was a gecko, a small green-and-black lizard, in her toothbrush holder on the first day we were there. It seemed to be living there. Andrea is not the sort of person who enjoys brushing her teeth with a toothbrush that has enjoyed close proximity to a small lizard. Lizards eat bugs.

On the kitchen wall there was a sign that warned: Be kind to the geckos. So I was. I tried to scoop up the bathroom gecko and reintroduce him to the great outdoors, but the lizard was perverse. He took a defensive stance and opened his mouth as if perfectly willing to take a tiny little chunk of me as he went down. I hesitated. But he was four inches long, tops, and I felt superior, so I scooped. He dove into the towels.

That night, after a few glasses of wine, I went out onto the lanai, turned on the outside light, and immediately began pulling insects from miles away. The light had drawn the insects, and the insects had drawn the geckos. Lizards the size of a finger and quite a few of them much larger. Black ones, green ones, red ones, white ones, all motionless on the wall. Waiting for the commuter train. An insect landed, the geckos froze, and suddenly one would swizzle over and clamp the insect in its jaws. It was like the best gladiator movie ever filmed, but on a ridiculously small budget. As long as the porch light stayed on there were new recruits.

Andrea did not like the geckos. She rousted them from her shoes, from underneath her bed, from behind wall paintings, from deep within her toothbrush cup, and from the corners of her closet. She persevered and maintained the only gecko-free room in the house. And thus was feasted on by the insects the geckos were trying to eat. So Andrea is not crazy about Hawaii.

My wife was next in line not to have fun in Hawaii. On the second morning, she dove into the water at a small beach and came up under a dead Portuguese man-of-war. At first, she noticed just a touch, a sensation, a vague unpleasantness. Within five minutes it was a faint pink mark. Ten minutes after that there were definite welts. And within a half hour she looked like she had been beaten with a horsewhip. She thought maybe we should start looking around for an emergency room before she went into shock for good.

The emergency room in Kauai was in a hospital on the other side of the island, connected by a two-lane road in the shape of a horseshoe, and there is only one road. The people in the emergency room showed her a book called *All Stings Considered* that contained pictures and descriptions of all the harmful flora and fauna of the island. Coral lacerations. Sharp, poisonous seaweed. Gelatinous sea creatures. There was a picture of a man who had jumped into the water on top of a Portuguese man-of-war. His testicles and thighs were black and swollen. His face was turned to the side and the eyes in the picture had been blacked out to preserve his anonymity. But you knew from his weary, slack expression that whatever vacation he had started was now effectively over.

My wife's vacation was now over, too. All of the water in Hawaii was now dangerous. She peered into crystal-clear, knee-deep water and debated wading in. Small, darting fish the size of a half-eaten carrot stick filled her with anxiety.

Hawaii was the last of the big-ass family vacations. With three girls sailing into college, we don't have the discretionary funds to blow on this kind of extravagance. Vacations have been rethought, trimmed down, pruned until a vacation has become a two-day concept, a long weekend, a meal and a drive along the beach.

The assistant librarian at another neighborhood branch is more vigilant about her vacation hours. Her name is Prianka, and she was the assistant librarian ten years ago when I was first hired. She showed me how to mend and rewrap books, how to write up the special convoluted receipt for a lost book, how to deal with abusive patrons, and how to minimize strife with whomever was the latest in the parade of senior librarians. "Heavy is the head that wears the crown," she'd say in an Indian accent, referring to the seniors.

Ten years later, she is still an assistant librarian, now at another branch. She was born in India, she is Hindu, and she is of a caste called Brahmin. The Indian part is apparent. She has worn a sari every day since she started working at the library. I have never seen her wear a skirt, dress, or pair of pants. She reads the news of India from appropriate Web sites, and she remembers stories of growing up in the Indian countryside, hot and rural, as if the whole world were Indian and hot and rural.

For lunch every day Prianka brings a Tupperware container of leftovers from the night before, and the leftovers always have a simple name like potatoes and peas or beans and chilies. Two minutes in the microwave and the smell wafts through the library, foreign and mouthwatering. If I ask her a few questions and appear curious, she gives me a bowl.

Recipe?

Recipe? she says. Oh, you don't need a recipe. Just potatoes and peas and a few spices. And that's where it all grinds to a stop for me. I know about things like salt and pepper, onion, garlic, some oregano, maybe cilantro and basil. Her list has much, much more, and she suggests a small Indian supermarket where I can get hold of these ingredients.

Because she is Hindu, there is no meat, no eggs, no animal fats, no beef boullion. Nothing that has ever lived in the animal realm. Butter and milk are acceptable because you don't have to slaughter the animal to get it. People bring in covered dishes for potlucks and special occasions, and she is cordial and enthusiastic but will decline. There are too many possibilities for folly. The healthiest-looking salad will have an egg, a slice of crumbled bacon, and a casserole is too odious to contemplate. She is not a Lutheran with vague, sprawling doubts. She is Hindu and she is vigilant on all fronts. It makes absolutely no difference to us, but it makes a difference to her. She shoulders this responsibility and never makes you feel like a lesser creature for believing otherwise.

Prianka has two daughters, born in India and raised from an early age in Bay City, California. The oldest one is now a doctor in New York State, and the youngest one is almost through with medical school at UCLA. Once the medical school bills are paid, Prianka intends to employ a rather pricey matchmaker and find both of her daughters husbands. What she would really like are two young men from India, doctors themselves, of an appropriate stature and class, who will relocate from India to wed her daughters in Southern California.

I am shocked, not so much that matchmaking is still a viable career in the world but that two California-raised girls, women, who have had access to MTV for the past ten years, would agree to such a thing. I, for example, once went out with the daughter of one of my mother's friends, but I was not pressured into marrying her, giving her many children, or stepping into a managerial role at her dad's shoe store. We went out once, had an okay time, and kissed each other a few times. I sensed that she wasn't let out of the house much and that she was green-lighting me just to have something to do on the weekends. But after one date, I was done. I did not enjoy being propelled through social encounters with someone's father's hand on my back. I preferred to ask out girls who had not read the bio and skimmed my annual report.

Prianka's vacation technique was much different than my own. Because she had worked for the city for such a long period of time, she didn't accrue vacation so much as amass it. When she finally announced her intention of flying back to India, she would take five weeks off. At the end of the allotted time, we'd get an overseas phone call. It was monsoon season. Hard to travel. She would be back in another three weeks or so. It all depended.

When Prianka is working at the library she never takes a day off. The curries burn off the flu, the garlic scares away the colds, and nothing else gets in the way of her perfect attendance. The rest of us wilt and fall under the attack of seasonal virus onslaughts, but Prianka does not waver. Day in, day out, year after year. Many years, she receives a special award for perfect attendance and a $25 gift card.

But when Prianka announces her biennial intention to visit family and friends on the Indian subcontinent, library administrators develop facial tics and stare at their wall calendars. They have to plan on Prianka being gone for an entire season. She has filled out the appropriate forms, asked for the time a year in advance, and she has more than enough vacation stockpiled. It doesn't matter that this creates scheduling problems for the library. Everything creates scheduling problems for the library. This is just on a grander scale.

Prianka recognizes the library's reluctance to grant vacations, so over the years she has trained administration to expect this periodical inconvenience. She is not partying it up on the Riviera, not sitting at a slot machine for twelve hours a day. She is making bread with female relatives in hundred-degree heat in a house where four-foot-long cobras sleep underneath the floorboards, where old men with skin like ruined parchment sleep out on the porch, waiting for the first large drop of rain to hit the courtyard in over six months and bring down the dust. Ask her and she will pull out the pictures, and even they seem hot.

Chapter Twenty-four
Flying Saucers and Lemon Squares

WHEN I WAS IN HIGH SCHOOL, I was in a small group of wretched, undateable nerds who played chess, listened to avant-garde music, hypnotized ourselves to see who we had been two hundred years ago, played Beatles albums backward to find out which one of them was really the Walrus, and wore McCarthy and McGovern for President lapel buttons until they became kitschy memorabilia. We followed flying-saucer news and were convinced there would be lots more of it if secret government agencies weren't suppressing the information on a daily basis. We went to conventions and sat through slide shows and presentations of grainy handheld cameras that documented the alien threat. Once a month, on a Friday, we would meet at someone's house and sit on a gently sloping roof, there under suburban Cleveland skies, looking for the truth. I did it until it seemed like a waste of time and a dumb thing to do. Even now, though, when I am walking my big, belligerent dog late at night, I look up and scan the heavens, hoping to redeem the lottery ticket I purchased nearly forty years ago. But I have moved on, to job and family and debt and layers of duty, and I no longer pin my hopes on discovering extraterrestrial life-forms. Though it would still be nice.

At our branch, we have an older patron just like this. Flying Saucer Man is like a lot of our regulars—he comes at the same time every day that we are open, for years. Then one day he is gone and we never see him again. In Flying Saucer Man's case, another patron who lives in the same neighborhood tells us that he finally had a stroke. An ambulance took him away in the middle of the night. He has gone from living independently to total institutionalization.

He is short, semi-dapper in his button-down, short-sleeved shirts, and he wears a generic baseball cap, the cap facing front, old-school style. He wears a cap because he is bald and because he is in the sun most of the day, walking. When he is not in the library, he is walking. He is healthy looking, if sunburned. He has a noticeable potbelly that does not seem in place with the rest of him. When I first met him, I thought he was in his late forties, but a neighbor who also remembers him corrects me and says he is in his late sixties. He always carries a pad and pencil to write down his observations, and his observations always seem to have something to do with life on other planets.

He gets on the library computers and downloads pictures of flying saucers, crop circles, glowing lights in the sky, aerial photos of deserted runways in the desert, and lurid sketches of sleek, amphibious-like craft plunging into the ocean. He pulls out a five-dollar bill and we break it into ones for him. He feeds the money into the printer and prints out inexpensive ink-jet copies of extraterrestrial spacecraft.

He says he gets these bundles of pictures together and sends them to a daughter of his in Norway. He is trying to convince her that the proof of alien visitation is not a spotty thing, not the product of similar, fevered minds, but overwhelming!

But he shakes his head sadly. "Doesn't matter what I do, though. She thinks I'm loony. Who knows, eh?"

For a moment, I imagine a Norwegian mailman hefting a large package from the United States, a bunch of loose pictures from the Internet with a common theme, a brief one-page letter in front to pull it all together. It feels like a mad, lonely thing, and I wonder if his daughter writes back, with pictures of her home, her husband, smiling little light-haired children, his grandchildren. Or does she open the package and make a few short, distressed Norwegian noises, wondering how on earth she can find the words to answer him. Or if she writes him back at all.

A few times he takes the time to explain his theories to me: the aliens are among us. They have certain markings to make themselves more plain to each other, eh? Sometimes one of their vehicles crashes, and when that happens the government—the U.S. government—rushes to the site and carts everything away. There are perfectly preserved aliens in underground compounds, sealed in glass pods. There are books of alien hieroglyphs that specialists work at night and day to decipher. There are videos out there of aliens walking stiffly through the desert, videos he has never seen, only heard about.

What could they want? he asks me, and I absolutely do not know. What could we tell them to make them understand? Will they ever accept us in their intergalactic embrace?

He tells me there is a radio program I simply have to listen to—it's at 3:30 in the morning, and he sets his alarm and sits in bed with a few pillows behind him, taking notes, jotting down the names of guests and authors, locations, Web sites, book titles, and home planets.

He is not a gregarious person—he is mostly lonely and unto himself. If you look at his pictures, he will reveal bits of himself, relax, and even laugh at himself a little. If he senses anything negative, mockery, he will gather up his pictures and set off for home, wherever that is. Or he will walk to another library, farther away, where he is not made to feel the troweled-on shame. He will begin putting together another package for a person halfway around the world who probably has almost no interest in receiving this package.

The last time I saw him I was driving to work. It was several blocks from the library. He was standing on the corner, shielding his eyes from the midmorning sun, watching a telephone repairman climb up a pole to work on the line. Maybe they were talking. About what I had no doubt. I bet you see a lot of funny stuff up there all day, eh?

188

Don Borchert

He looked fairly content, as if he were critiquing the scene. He had his pad and his pencil and the day was crisp and clear. I waved to him as I drove past, beeped my horn, and he raised his hand in acknowledgment, but I could tell by the look on his face that he didn't recognize me out of the context of the library. And he didn't recognize the car.

He didn't come into the library that day.

He never came in again.

We have another patron who has also been coming in regularly for the past several years. She is at least seventy, wears orthopedic shoes, and is known in the library for her stylish collection of fine women's hats. Her name is Mrs. Aida Cripp. A taxi brings her to the library at least once a week. When she is through, we make a phone call for her and another taxi comes and takes her back home.

She says she loves to bake, but her children have grown and moved away, out of the state. There is no way she can consume the things she makes. Could we do her a favor? Could she drop off a tray of cookies every now and then? A linzer torte? Brownies? Pumpkin-bran muffins? Apple pan dowdy? Raspberry squares? Some simple butter cookies? Otherwise, it makes no sense for her to bake—she'd just be throwing them out at the end. And what's the point of that?

She confides in me, "I know how the world is. Some strange woman coming in off the street and she wants you to eat something . . . no way! People are crazy, believe me, I know! I'm afraid to answer my phone anymore. They know my name and they want me to buy things! But I assure you, my lemon squares are just flour, sugar, butter, lemon zest, and a few other things."

I tell her, no problem. "We'll give a few to the pages and keep an eye on them. If they're still standing at the end of their shift, we're all set."

She smiles. She likes a little flirting.

"You are awful," she says. So the next time she comes in, she brings a large tray of lemon squares. They smell warm and sweet and lemony. I eat one of them at the reference desk—usually one of the bigger sins in the library demeanor manual. Thank god it is the middle of the day and the schools aren't out yet. Henry sees me eating while he is working on his crossword puzzle, but he doesn't seem to mind. In any case, he doesn't begin muttering to himself, which is always a good sign.

Mrs. Cripp is very pleased. "I should get out of here before you pass out." Hee, hee, hee. A little color comes to her cheeks.

Every week, Mrs. Cripp comes in, a different flowered hat on her head, and every few weeks she brings in a bag or a tray of baked goods. She is an incredible baker, and we are the "good eaters" she had been hoping for.

Several months later, in the rain and gloom of November, Mrs. Cripp calls the library. She is bedridden, nothing to worry about, nothing serious, but she doesn't want to chance it with too much activity. There is a tray of cherry-granola bars cooling in her kitchen, and she doesn't want them to go to waste. She has called her regular cabdriver and he has offered to deliver them.

Forty-five minutes later, the cabdriver comes in, a little puzzled, with a tray of cherry-granola bars. We offer him one. His eyebrows go up in bemusement. Maybe it's distrust. No thanks, he says.

On Valentine's Day, Terri buys a card and we all sign it. Mrs. Cripp opens the card and is a little embarrassed. For gosh sakes, they're just cookies. Goodness, it's no big deal. Just some sifted flour and vanilla extract, brown sugar, molasses, unsalted butter, almonds, lemon zest, and a few other things.

Chapter Twenty-five
Senior Librarians

MY CAREER AS A CIVIL SERVANT, even taking into consideration my utter lack of advancement, has been totally the result of fortuitous accident. I started as an assistant librarian more than a dozen years ago, and have remained one. For those eyeing the position of senior librarian, however, the road is not accidental at all. It is long, arduous, and deliberate. Senior librarians have positions with the most latitude, are the highest paid and most educated, and have an array of prosaic, redundant, largely bureaucratic responsibilities that make it one of the most suffocating, joyless ways to make a living on the planet. When an angry patron threatens to take it to the mayor's office, a wary senior librarian must deal with him. If the senior cannot mollify the patron and the patron thinks he will just drive over to City Hall and throw a fit, the mortar in a senior's career turns to dust. Being an administrator who can't resolve conflict is no way to be known to high-ranking city officials. So they mollify.

Seniors are also in charge of employee dismissals and yearly performance reviews. Both take inordinate amounts of paperwork. You can't just hire or fire someone and let the chips fall where they may, and you can't on a whim put a brief note into the employee file every now and then saying they're doing a pretty darn good job. Each piece of paperwork must lock into every other piece of paperwork like a complicated jigsaw puzzle. Seniors must learn to damn an employee without appearing to be emotional, judgmental, or biased, and they must praise their employees with a hint of rot in the tone, so they don't look foolish down the road when the employee starts to go bad.

Seniors are a lonely sort, cast into a role where they are constantly interacting with the public. They cannot bond with the rank-and-file employees they govern. They can share a morning doughnut and stand around talking about last night's television shows like they're just one of the gang, but it is all a charade and a courtesy on both parts. Their specialized education and attendant duties make them a different breed, and they may truly bond only with other seniors.

The seniors have regular, mandatory meetings to cement this bond. Every two weeks they meet in the basement of the main branch in a windowless room to talk about what needs to be talked about, to go over changes in procedure, to debate legislature that affects the library, to review new books, and to judiciously trash-talk about whoever isn't there.

These meetings have been going on since the 1940s and are still essentially the same. Every senior will sooner or later complain about what an utter waste of time they are. They sit around a large wooden table. Everyone has a fort of loose papers, reviews, new books, and steaming coffee containers in front of them. The doughnuts are put out and a discussion begins. It swells and goes on until everyone has contributed and it is talked out. Then they move on to the next topic.

Rarely are decisions made. Decisions are made by people in City Hall, not the library. The seniors are just voicing their encouragement, dissent, or outrage. They are also seeing who is with them on a certain point and who is a'gin them. At the end of this segment of the meeting, the seniors bring out their order cards and take turns reading what other seniors hope will be brief reviews of many, many new books. Some of the reviews are copied from magazines, some are pulled from the Internet, and some of them are original. The seniors are trying to interest other seniors in their own favorite genres. Juanita, for example, is all over feminist literature and contemporary Latino fiction.

The availability of point and click e-mail should have driven a stake in this dated affair years ago, but it has not. The senior meeting lives on, another curious affectation as timely and relevant as buggy whips and boutonnieres on shop clerks.

Over the years, Juanita has made enemies at the senior meetings. She wants to do too much, too quickly, without enough calm reflection and study. She seems to refuse to acknowledge the unwritten hierarchy within the library, although it is obvious to everyone else. Juanita started out as an after-school page at one of the branches fewer than ten years earlier, went away to UC Davis, and came back to Southern California a newly minted librarian. She's had a few other jobs before this, and stayed at each one long enough to springboard on to the next. Juanita has a number of defenders, and they argue that people don't know how to take her because she is young and full of ideas, and ambitious, and older librarians may not be comfortable around this combination of strengths. Several former allies are stunned, however, at the alacrity and precision with which Juanita seems to wheel and turn on them. From a united front with Juanita in the vanguard, all of a sudden they are out in the cold, exposed, friendless, and vulnerable. What they had construed as an alliance and as friendship was the manipulation of . . . a patsy! They had not only been used but hustled! Manipulated!

Juanita does not seem to worry about the carnage. She thinks she is not being promoted as fast as she should be because of the glass ceiling. She is a woman, and an attractive one, she'd like to add. It is a disingenuous argument because the seniors are almost all women. She is a firebrand amongst the woman, a wounded doe with the men. Most of the time, though not all, the ploy works. Even when it doesn't, no one wants to take a stand publicly against Juanita and be on her shit list. She has a long memory for people who have taken positions contrary to her own, and her attitude toward them changes. She is still publicly bright and effusive toward these people, but later—in private—she will confess grave doubts about their abilities, their talents, and their commitment. When these people reappear, she is bright and effusive again. The dark clouds have been blown away and it's going to be a nice day after all. It is kind of a shame to see such bald-faced, naked Machiavellian talents squandered in the civil service, where there are such limited, measured gains in throwing your comrades-in-arms to the dogs.

Lillian, the senior librarian, begins working at my branch after Juanita is promoted to the main library. They soon become friends. This concerns some of Lillian's other librarian friends, who fear that Juanita has a predilection for turning feral. When Juanita secures a famous children's writer to make a presentation at her branch, Lillian agrees to drive over and help with crowd control. When Lillian the senior librarian puts together a presentation celebrating multicultural-ism at *her* branch, Juanita will jump in right at the last moment—no matter how busy she is—and shoulder 50 percent of the credit for put-ting together such an ambitious program. Afterward, Juanita and Lil-lian will get together for a rare girls-night-out, to toast their success and get a little frisky. They will gab at a neighborhood bar like teenagers, talking about this and that. Lillian is naturally a spigot of information for Juanita and a second set of eyes. Oh, girlfriend, he did not say that! I don't believe it! What else did he say?

Lillian naturally is just glad to have made a friend.

Lillian is more than a little shy, and she openly, sincerely ad-mires Juanita's brassy, in-your-face style and confrontational nature. She would like to be more like that herself, but such a thing is un-natural for her. She hopes to be able to pick it up from Juanita, like the lyrics to a particularly difficult song.

Lillian underestimates her own considerable talents. She thinks she is merely adequate, but she is calm, articulate, and good in the many small crises that befall a branch library on an almost weekly basis. She can empathize with an angry patron but refuse to be cowed. She takes her job seriously and tries to be a good example for everyone else at the branch. She is up-to-date on the paperwork, the grant proposals, the work orders about malfunctioning thermostats and sparking fluorescent light fixtures, the employee time cards, the performance reviews, the incident reports, the quarterly reports to administration, the book reviews, the weeding projects, the volunteer statistics sheets, the running annual budget for the branch *and* the amended annual budget for the branch, the capital expenditure forms, the requests to the Friends for additional computers and furniture, and anything else that finds its way to her large and mounded in-basket.

The reason she went into the profession in the first place was books. She still remembers the effect a certain book can have on people at the right time in their lives. A book, at its most mundane, can be a loaded gun. At its most powerful, it can split the trunk of a tree, mend a broken heart, heal the sick, and topple a corrupt government.

Lillian's two areas of specialty are nonfiction books concerning survival in extraordinary circumstances and Christian fiction. The memoirs of a man trapped beneath an avalanche of snow. A fictional account of a Christian family wending their way West in a covered wagon. How a World War II seaman managed to stay alive on the open Atlantic for sixty-five days with only a tin cup, a magnifying glass, and a broken wristwatch.

Or how a World War II seaman survived on the high seas for sixty-five days with only a tin cup, a dog-eared Bible, and a desire to know God.

Christian fiction.

It's getting to be big business, this Christian fiction, but it is mostly second-rate crap with generic plots, innocuous, pastel cover art, and two-dimensional characters hawking nondenominational, two-dimensional beliefs. It is the next big thing in the library, a genre that was nonexistent just five years ago. If you are currently unemployed or behind in your rent, you would be advised to start writing Christian fiction, and you should probably start before everyone else does.

But Lillian the senior librarian cannot waste too much time recommending disaster books and Christian fiction—there's too much paperwork to do, and ah, there's the rub. For Lillian got into the library thing because she loved books. Being an administrator, they put some paperwork in front of her that had to be done before she did anything else. Because she was diligent with the paperwork, they gave her more, so she did that, too. Eventually, it got to the point where patron interruptions annoyed her and kept her from completing her paperwork.

There's also the problem of ambition. If you're young and have the eye of the tiger, you'd like more. More of whatever there is. In the world of the library, more can mean dominion over several branches, an increased say in discretionary budget, a voice at the city council meetings, or any one of a number of big fish/small pond perks. But "more" is probably not why any of the senior librarians became senior librarians. It is a ridiculous field to get into if you prize ambition — Juanita being the obvious exception.

When she first took the job at my branch, it was because we were a bit of a challenge. The kids were exhausting and it seemed like we were relinquishing control. There was almost no relationship with the nearby schools. There were several exploding populations of ethnicities who were minimally and inadequately served. The police were openly tired of responding to our complaints, and the branch was in such turmoil that many of the senior, full-time employees would transfer to different branches as soon as an opportunity presented itself.

Juanita called me into her office once and asked me what my career goal was — had I ever thought of going back to college and getting a degree in library science? She said she didn't think it would be that difficult for me. The classes were in the evenings, twice a week. It would take a few years. I told her it would be impossible for me to go back to school. Higher education had scarred me for life. I never wanted to take a class again, much less walk into a class prepared for a midterm or final. Damn shame, she said.

Juanita finally ran into too many dead ends at the main branch and took a job as the chief of staff for libraries in a small college town in Wisconsin. To many, it appeared she relocated for ego rather than money. Lillian organized two going-away parties, one at the main library, another, smaller one at her own home. Juanita, her husband, and her new baby boy got out of Los Angeles at the right time—the real estate market was going crazy. They made enough from the sale of their home to buy the house in Wisconsin outright, and there was enough left over to set her husband up with a small Starbucks-like franchise. They moved in early January.

Leaving Lillian all alone. She and Juanita relied on daily e-mails and late-night telephone calls.

By the first week of May Lillian had rewritten her résumé and was beginning to send it out. In a brief e-mail of encouragement, Juanita said she was very proud of Lillian. By July Lillian had accepted a position as the head of reference services for a library system in northern San Diego. The pay was about the same but the responsibilities were different. More varied. It felt like an upward move.

Chapter Twenty-six
Special Events

TERRI HAS COME IN on a Saturday morning to oversee her first big event of the school year, based on the "Series of Unfortunate Events" books by Lemony Snicket. There are going to be crafts, games, puzzles, coloring sheets, and small prizes that will be won by whomever walks through the front door—in other words, everyone. Terri is getting over a bad cold and would rather be at home in bed, but she feels obliged to come in and run the thing. She feels she is under the magnifying glass because she is relatively new to the job, not that anyone would begrudge her taking the time off to get well. But there is only one children's librarian per branch, and no one else in our library would really know how to run the event. Also, the Friends of the Library have kindly kicked in some money for prizes and snacks, and prizes and snacks always guarantee a nice crowd. Terri tells me that she is hoping the achy, fevery, exhausted thing will go away for a few hours, and she will eventually be able to go back home, turn on some music, and fall asleep in bed with all the blankets on.

But there is a problem, and a worrisome one.

For some reason, the main branch has released two different flyers for the event. One of them states that the event will start at 2 p.m.—which is the time Terri had planned on—and the other has the event starting at 4 p.m. For years, the main branch has printed flyers without any kind of proofreading built into the process, and they see inaccuracies, misprints, and bad spelling as a natural part of life. Not everyone has taken up this happy-go-lucky attitude. When our branch sees a flyer that announces

**Come to the Bay City Library
for an afternoon of storys and carfts!
Call (310) 373-841 for further details!**

we try to get every copy of the flyer we can so we can throw them in the trash and print up our own. It can be depressing to think the general public sees you as a group of well-dressed, nicely mannered idiots. Even the WILL WORK FOR FOOD guys seem to take more pride in their work. Not us. When we receive bundles of the latest library flyer, we scan them gravely, like a doctor checking a patient's X-ray for dark spots. We are not optimistic.

The flyers for this promotion were eventually corrected, but Terri has an ugly feeling that a second group of kids will begin piling into the library shortly after the first event is over. If this happens, she will have to put the drop cloths back on the table, pull the craft supplies back out, and do the whole thing again. She will not be responsible for disappointing a group of young children—especially on the day of her *first* big event of the school year.

Her husband drove her to work earlier, but he is worried about her. Curtis thinks she is exhausted and that this might be the thing that will make her health nosedive in general. His opinion: let someone else run the event. It is, after all, simple crafts with glue and cloth and paper and simple games. Let it be a success without her.

At 1:30 p.m. Terri is sitting in the back room, sipping an energy drink that does not seem to be working, trying to muster her resources. Everything has been set up, and the first sprinkling of kids is beginning to come in with their mothers and fathers. Economics in the neighborhood being what they are, a simple, free program always pulls people into the library. The maverick, homeschooled kids and their right-wing Christian moms might also drop in—if the program doesn't sound too seditious or make any references to devils, spells, witches, wizards, or the supernatural. Homeschooling moms can be a skittish lot, and if the name "Harry Potter" is even whispered, their ears stand up and they bolt like high-strung gazelles catching the first scent of a hungry lion.

By 1:45 p.m., the back of the library is awash with small children, noisy and eager for something to happen. The theme of the program has to do with a series of books by Lemony Snicket, but most of the kids are too young to know that. They just know they have been promised a good time. Terri moves into the area, doling out hugs to the kids she's met before, thanking the parents for coming, and announces that it will all begin soon, soon. A few more minutes pass, but the program has to begin on time, not a moment early. Because we're in the Los Angeles area, we can count on about 20 percent of the crowd arriving fashionably late, a cultural eccentricity we might as well blame on those zany, world-weary Lakers and Dodgers fans—arriving late, leaving early, as if the whole thing was an ordeal to be minimized, like Thanksgiving at a crotchety relative's house.

Some of the parents will come in forty-five minutes late for what is billed as an hour program. I wonder why they even bother. When you pull out of the driveway at 2:35 p.m. for a program that starts at 2 p.m., how are you not setting your child up for a taste of disappointment?

At 1:50, the whole library is humming with noise and activity, and as Terri walks past a row of juvenile paperbacks she sees Crystal, a short fifth-grade, curly-haired, freckled redhead who usually follows Terri around the library after school like a baby quail. Immediately, something is not right. She seems to be curled up, in a fetal position, hiding, her lips are quivering, her teeth are chattering, and her face is pale and wild with tears.

She sees Terri and flies to her, grabbing and pulling Terri to her, not the happy, sunny girl she was the week before, but sobbing, afraid, almost hysterical. She clings to Terri, can't talk, and it's not just a ploy for attention.

Terri takes her into the back room to find a little privacy and Crystal starts sobbing. Terri tells her calm down, honey, calm down, stroking her hair, not knowing what else to do, and it is 1:58 p.m.

Terri sends out a library page to tell the crowd, "The program will start in five minutes! Five minutes everyone!" The parents don't care. The kids don't care. Terri is just buying a few minutes. The overall noise level in the library gets a little higher.

When Crystal calms down and is finally able to talk, she tells Terri that her stepfather has been angry with her mother again. Things have been getting worse and worse the past few days. This morning, he was reading the newspaper at the kitchen table, and finally he threw a plate and a hot cup of coffee at Crystal's mom. Then he got up from his chair and came at her, started slapping her, and she swung back once to drive him back, hitting him so hard and unexpectedly in the chin that his teeth clicked together. He went wild and started slapping and punching her, following her from room to room, beating her, throwing things at her, calling her horrible names.

Crystal's mom has already spoken to Crystal about this kind of thing, like a family who has rehearsed earthquake drills. She told her that if things ever got out of hand—and out of hand was not exactly defined—Crystal was not to intervene. She was to flee, go some place safe, and call the police. Call 911, give them the address, and tell them to hurry. Her mom's luck with men was not so good. Crystal tells Terri that she had a feeling something like this was coming.

Crystal opened the front door to her apartment and hesitated. Part of her felt she was abandoning her mother. And then the stepfather whirled, saw Crystal standing in the open doorway, and hissed that when he was done with Crystal's mother, they both knew who he was going to come after next—Crystal!

Crystal ran out of the house, fleeing a nightmare. She did not run to the neighbor's house, because she didn't really have any kind of relationship with any of the neighbors. The stepfather didn't want them talking to the neighbors and would get mad if she even stopped and said hello to them. She did not run to a friend's house, because she had a feeling he would follow her there and terrorize them all. So she ran two blocks to the public library and was hiding in the juvenile paperback books because that was all she could think of doing.

Terri calls the police, and the police dispatcher tells Terri to keep Crystal in the library—don't let her go back home!—and that a squad car will roll by as soon as they buttoned up the stepfather situation.

Terri suggests that Crystal sit in the back room and read a book until the police come. The thought of being left alone terrifies Crystal. She fears that as soon as she is left alone, her stepfather will peer at her through a window, smile at his luck, force the door, and do something horrible before anyone can help.

It is just after 2 p.m.

Terri has an idea born of desperation. She has to do a program. Would Crystal be her assistant? Crystal smiles for the first time, wipes her nose with her arm, and says okay.

Terri and Crystal start the Lemony Snicket program at 2:11. While Terri reads passages from a book, Crystal stands next to her, arms folded, listening. When they come to the crafts part of the program, Crystal and Terri go from table to table and help the preschoolers with their crayons and glue and glitter. Eventually, Crystal stays at one table to help a child who seems to need a lot of extra help, and Terri moves ahead, alone. Crystal is a conscientious helper. All the children are pleased with the results of their crafts.

During refreshments, two policemen and a policewoman show up and ask to speak to Crystal in private. Crystal tells Terri she is okay now and goes into the back room again to give a formal statement.

A social worker with a kind of battered leather attaché case also shows up and, after speaking to Crystal and to the police, asks Terri for a statement. The social worker is very warm and reassuring, telling Crystal that one of the police officers will take her home whenever she'd like—the police have taken the stepfather somewhere to settle down, and he won't be putting a key in their front door anytime soon.

After Crystal leaves, the social worker tells Terri something else she did not know. When they asked Crystal why she ran the two blocks to the public library instead of running to a neighbor's door, Crystal told them that the library was the only place she felt safe. It was quiet and safe in the library, and even if it wasn't always quiet it was still safe.

The time is now 3:45 p.m.

By now Terri feels like laying down on the floor in the abysmal employee break room and dissolving into the miserable carpeting. Her legs feel heavy, her head feels heavy, she has a headache, her physical resources have fallen dangerously close to zero, and she has begun to lose her voice—a sign that her body has had enough. Her hands are caked with dried glue and there are smears of glitter on her face.

Looking out into the library, it is just as she had suspected. A smaller group of preschoolers has begun to trickle into the library, uniformly excited and happy. And why not? There's going to be a craft! And prizes! By 4 p.m. there are fourteen kids in the library, the noise level begins to swell once more, and Terri gets off the floor and goes out to do the whole thing again. The kids laugh and giggle at the glitter on her face, as if it were part of the program. They can't wait to do the same! How cosmopolitan!

By 5:15 p.m., the program is over—again—the remaining kids have wolfed down the remaining refreshments, and the library is Closed for the day. The kids hold up their crafts proudly and wave good-bye to Terri as they go out the front door. And then they are out and the library is empty. Terri and the staff survey the carnage. There is glitter everywhere—even the potted houseplants near the activity are shimmering with the stuff. One of the staff suggests leaving the whole mess until Monday morning and the motion is seconded and carried.

A week later, Terri is once again regaining her voice, and she shows me a $25 employee award she has been given by library administration for persistence under fire. The $25 is a nice gesture. It's good to get some recognition, especially when you're a little insecure in the job. What warms Terri's heart, however, is Crystal's statement to the social worker: that she went to the one place she could think of where she felt really safe. The public library.

Terri does not want to think about it too much or in too much depth. We are all a little too calloused and cynical. You might as well state you only feel truly safe in a bus station, a baseball stadium, or the post office. Or standing next to a high-speed metal lathe in a busy machine shop.

But this is where Crystal ran. Terri feels good about the job she did, and good about the institution she works for. It is a good feeling that will last longer than the $25 award. It will buoy her up in the times to come when she feels unappreciated, overworked, or simply ignored by the people and the city she works for. It gives her a handle on why she got into this line of work.

In the end, she will probably use the $25 to buy more craft supplies. The jar of glitter is dangerously low.

Afterword

MY BRANCH LIBRARY HAS BEEN changing lately, so much so that it's hard to keep up with it. Several more senior librarians have come and gone. Our branch is the elfish forge to see what kind of stuff the senior librarians are made of. Terri has been promoted to the main branch, although she would disagree and say it was merely a lateral move. She'd be wrong, though. The main branch has more funds, more staffing, more programs, and more patrons. It is the big leagues in our library system. When school started in the fall, Terri's young fans were stunned to find her gone. Many bit their lips and wept. Months later, the older ones still come up once or twice a week and ask, "Have you talked to her? When is she coming back? Did she ask about me?" The younger ones have forgotten what she looks like, and they hang out at the reference desk, asking the new children's librarian if she has any pets.

Our branch has a brand-new Homework Center in the middle of the library, near the reference desk. There are new chairs, new desks, new computers loaded with age-specific educational software, a stash of school textbooks and school supplies, access to staplers, tape dispensers, calculators, and unlimited color printing. Some new procedures are going to have to be hammered together. Presently, the Homework Center is ripe for abuse. In the beginning, we were going through five hundred color copies a day. Kids were printing out MySpace profiles, manga characters, pictures of Bart Simpson, cheats to video games, and dozens and dozens of photographs of adorable dogs and cats available at the local shelter. We have school volunteers overseeing the printers but it's too much even for them.

The Homework Center is for kids only. Adults who want to horn in and print out their résumés are shunted to the public terminals in front of the library. They are shocked that they do not have access to the same free resources. If they are petulant and threaten to complain the city officials are ready for them.

The city's best idea was implementing a group called the park rangers, and they were an immediate hit. They are the next best thing to police, and for a fraction of the cost. They are city employees, young men, trained in mediating and negotiating, and they wear distinctive T-shirts and jackets that identify themselves. They do not carry guns or tasers or wear anything resembling paramilitary attire. They do not make arrests. Even so, they are a calming and reassuring presence, perhaps because no one is completely sure what they can or can't do. They patrol public areas in the city like playgrounds, parks, and the public library. They come into the library almost every day after school for a quick walk around. On the days they don't actually enter the building, they sit in the parking lot out front for a while just to gauge the activity.

All these changes—the Homework Center, the rangers—may be for nothing. Soon, our library will be closing for a complete retrofit. How long we stay closed is hard to say. The contractor's reticence to commit to a timetable makes us think it will be a while. By the time we open back up again, the middle school across the street will be closed down for the summer. At the beginning of the next school year, it will cease to be a public school, and all the students will be required to go somewhere else. Eventually, the school will be torn down and, some time in the distant future, rebuilt. Or the funds will dry up, and it will sit, boarded up, an empty school across the street from a public library that was finally getting a handle on what to do with all the kids.

A few weeks ago, I was taking some trash out to the Dumpster in back of the library and one of the middle-school boys was there, crying, holding an empty shoe box in his hands. He was a regular in the library named Tyler. I had never known a Tyler before in my life until I started working at the library. Now I know half a dozen of them.

"What's going on, Tyler?"

He held up the shoe box. "My rat got out. I forgot to keep the top on. Now he's back behind the Dumpster and I can't get him out. He's scared."

Poor kid. I go back into the library but I'm not exactly sure what I'm looking for. Newspapers? A yardstick? A coat hanger I can take apart to give the thing a poke? By the time I come back outside, Tyler is off running, chasing the rat around the corner of the building. When it makes the turn, it scampers up the brick edifice of the library and stops by the eaves of the building, twelve or thirteen feet from the ground. Other kids begin to congregate. Some of the boys suggest throwing rocks and clods of dirt at the rodent until it loses its footing. I shake my head no. Some of the girls take this opportunity to scream. It is, after all, a rat. It begins to resemble a staged reenactment of *Lord of the Flies*.

One of the park rangers appears out of nowhere and goes to his car for a pair of leather gloves. He is a nice young guy, and a proud father with a recent baby of his own. He figures this is one of the things he will have to do in years to come. One of the library pages, Jose, agrees to get the stepladder that Mr. Weams's janitorial crew keeps in the locked closet to change out the fluorescent lights. I go to the back of the library to retrieve the abandoned shoe box. A lot of the kids inside the library are now pouring out to take part in the chaos. It is turning into an after-school Mardi Gras.

When I come back with the shoe box, I notice for the first time that Tyler is no longer in the crowd.

"Where's Tyler?" I ask one of the calmer girls who is in the same grade.

"Which one?" she replies.

I wave the shoe box. "The Tyler who owns the rat."

She grins. "His mom just picked him up."

I am bewildered. "What about his rat?"

She shakes her pretty head. "That's not really Tyler's rat. It's just a rat he found in the street on the way to school. I think it's sick. It was making all kinds of weird noises. Teacher wouldn't let him bring it out of the box."

It is a sewer rat with some kind of illness.

The park ranger is smiling, halfway up the ladder, a pair of leather gloves on his hands. Jose is holding the base of the ladder to keep it steady.

As I'm about to warn the park ranger about what is probably a disease-ridden rat, another car pulls into the parking lot of the library. It is a family, a young man and woman and a small child. They are all smiling, happy to be here, and for a moment I see it as they must see it—a crowd of happy, carefree children and earnest, conscientious adults watching over them, playing, working, getting along, out in the sun. Taking care of business. It is a very appealing picture.

And almost true.

Bibliography

THE DEWEY DECIMAL NUMBER of each book follows its entry below, in parentheses. These books can be found at the same spot at all libraries using the Dewey numbering system. Although works of fiction do have their own Dewey numbers, our library system classifies them separately, alphabetically by the author's last name.

Introduction

Trumble, Kelly. *The Library of Alexandria.* New York: Clarion Books, 2003. (J 027.032 T)

Brand, Max. *The Fastest Draw.* Boston: G.K. Hall, 1989.

Max Brand (1892–1944) wrote as many as 500 westerns. Real name was Frederick Schiller Faust. Other pseudonyms included: George O. Baxter, Evin Evans, David Manning, Peter Dawson, John Frederick, Pete Morland, Nicholas Silver, Frederick Furst, and Dennis Lawton.

Chapter One: A Civil Servant Is Born

Sethna, Dhun H. *Classical Music for Everybody: A Companion to Good Listening.* Sierra Madre, California: Fitzwilliam Press, 1997. (780.15 S495)

Cassell, Julian. *Do-It-Yourself Home Improvement: A Step-By-Step Guide*. New York: Dorling Kindersley, 2006. (643.7 C344)

Levine, Nathan. *Typing and Keyboarding for Everyone: 35 Easy Lessons to Improve Speed and Accuracy*. Lawrenceville, New Jersey: Thomson/Arco, 2002. (652.3 L665tk)

Chapter Two: A First Taste of the Library

Meltzer, Milton. *Brother, Can You Spare a Dime: The Great Depression, 1929–1933*. New York: Random House, 1973. (973.916 M528)

Pearson, Roberta E. *The Many Lives of the Batman: Critical Approaches to a Superhero and His Media*. New York: Routledge, 1991. (741.509 M295)

Weller, Sam. *Bradbury Chronicles: The Life of Ray Bradbury*. New York: William Morrow, 2005. (813 B798w)

Chapter Three: My First Year

Silver, Gerald. *Understanding Computers*. New York: Harper Perennial, 1994. (004 S587)

De Caux, Len. *Labor Radical: From the Wobblies to CIO, A Personal History*. Boston: Beacon Press, 1970. (331.88 D291)

Comfort, Alex. *The Joy of Sex*. New York: Crown Publishers, 2002. (613.96 C732)

Chapter Four: How It Used to Be

Puls, Mark. *Samuel Adams: Father to the American Revolution*. New York: Palgrave Macmillan, 2006. (B A217p)

Chapter Five: The Reference Desk

Kelley Blue Book Official Guide for Older Cars. Costa Mesa,
California: Kelley Blue Book, 2007. (KBB.com)

Gray, Henry. *Gray's Anatomy: The Anatomical Basis of Medicine
and Surgery.* New York: Churchill Livingstone, 1995.
(611 G779)

Holzer, Harold (editor). *Lincoln-Douglas Debates: The First
Complete, Unexpurgated Text.* New York: Harper Collins, 1993.
(973.68 L736l)

Chapter Six: Illegal Activity

Schliefer, Jay. *Methamphetamine: Speed Kills.* New York: Rosen
Publishers, 1999. (J 362.299 S)

McCloskey, Robert. *Make Way for Ducklings.* New York: Viking,
1969.

Chapter Seven: The Civil Servant's Cycle of Life

Swisher, Karin. *What Is Sexual Harassment?* San Diego,
California: Greenhaven Press, 1995. (305.42 W555)

Armstrong, Elizabeth. *America's 100 Best Places to Retire.*
Houston, Texas: Vacation Publications, 2003. (646.79 A512)

Ezekiel, Raphael S. *The Racist Mind: Portraits of Neo-Nazis and
Klansmen.* New York: Viking, 1995. (305.8 E99)

Chapter Eight: A Library Page

Arthur, Diane. *Recruiting, Interviewing, Selecting and Orienting
New Employees.* New York: AMACOM, 2006. (658.311 A788)

Levy, Steven. *Hackers: Heroes of the Computer Revolution.*
Garden City, New York: Anchor, 1984. (001.642 L668)

Burton, Dreena. *Everyday Vegan: Recipes and Lessons for Living
the Vegan Life.* Vancouver: Arsenal Pulp Press, 2001. (641.5636
B974)

Chapter Nine: The Parent Conference

Brokaw, Brian. *Pokemon Trading Card Game Player's Guide.*
Lahaina, Maui: Sandwich Islands Publications, 1999.
(J 794.8 B)

Dudley, William. *Vietnam War: Opposing Viewpoints.* San Diego,
California: Greenhaven Press, 1998. (959.7043 V666Qo)

Greenwood, Marie. *Barbie: A Visual Guide to the Ultimate
Fashion Doll.* London: Dorling Kindersley, 2003. (J 745.592 B)

Chapter Ten: The Graduates

Scotts Specialized Catalogue of United States Stamps. Sidney,
Ohio: Scott Publishing Company. Annual. (769.56 S431U)

Kaeser, Gigi. *Of Many Colors: Portraits of Multi-Racial Families.*
Amherst: University of Massachusetts Press, 1997. (306.846
K11)

Hoy, David. *College Financial Aid: The Best Resource to Help
You Find the Money.* Seattle, Washington: Resource Pathways,
1998. (378.3 C697h)

Chapter Eleven: Overdue Fines and Fees

Chilton's Guide to Chassis Electronics and Power Accessories.
Radner, Pennsylvania: Chilton Book Co., 1989. (629.254
C538)

Shangle, Barbara. *California Missions.* Beaverton, Oregon:
American Products Co., 1997. (979.402 S528)

Thucydides. *The Peloponnesian War.* Chicago: University of
Chicago Press, 1989. (938.05 T532)

Webster, Richard. *Numerology Magic: Use Number Squares
for Love, Luck, & Protection.* St. Paul, Minnesota: Llewellyn
Publications, 1998. (133.43 W383)

Chapter Twelve: Wild Animals in the Library

Summers, Marc. *Everything in Its Place: My Trials and Triumphs
with Obsessive Compulsive Disorder.* New York: J.P. Tarcher/
Putnam, 1999. (616.8522 S955)

Grace, Catherine O'Neill. *Dogs on Duty.* Washington, D.C.:
National Geographic Society, 1988. (J 636.708 O)

Kalstone, Shirlee. *Allergic to Pets?* New York: Bantam Books,
2006. (616.97 K14)

Chapter Thirteen: The Friends of the Library

Anderson, Luther A. *How to Hunt American Small Game.* New
York: Funk & Wagnalls, 1969. (799.25 A547)

Chapter Fourteen: Volunteers

Swinger, Marlys. *Sing Through the Day: Eighty Songs for Children*. Farmington, Pennsylvania: Plough Publishing House, 1999. (J 784.62S)

Gillespie, Kellie M. *Teen Volunteer Services in Libraries*. Lanham, Maryland: VOYA Books, 2004. (021.2 G478)

Lee, Henry. *Advances in Fingerprint Technology*. Boca Raton, Florida: CRC Press, 1994. (363.258 A244)

Chapter Fifteen: The Renaissance Patron

Benson, Michael. *Encyclopedia of the JFK Assassination*. New York: Facts on File, 2002. (973.922 B474)

Sussman, Julie. *Dare to Repair Plumbing*. New York: Collins, 2005. (696.1 S964)

Hunter, Susan S. *AIDS in America*. New York: Palgrave Macmillan, 2006. (362.1969 H947)

Chapter Sixteen: Card Registrations

Fox, Loren. *Enron: The Rise and Fall*. Hoboken, New Jersey: Wiley, 2003. (333.79 F792)

Plimmer, Martin. *Beyond Coincidence: Stories of Amazing Coincidence and the Mystery and Mathematics Behind Them*. New York: Thomas Dunne Books, 2006. (031.02 P728)

Chapter Seventeen: Cinco de Mayo

Yoon, In-Jin. *On My Own: Korean Businesses and Race Relations in America*. Chicago: University of Chicago Press, 1997. (338.6422 Y59)

Modarres, Ali. *The Racial and Ethnic Structure of Los Angeles County: A Geographic Guide*. Los Angeles: Edmund G. "Pat" Brown Institute of Public Affairs, California State University, Los Angeles, 1994. (305.8 M689)

Vaca, Nick Corona. *The Presumed Alliance: The Unspoken Conflict Between Latinos and Blacks and What It Means for America*. New York: Rayo, 2004. (305.868 V112)

Chapter Eighteen: MMM

Slote, Stanley J. *Weeding Library Collections: Library Weeding Methods*. Englewood, Colorado: Libraries Unlimited, 1997. (025.216 S634)

Dennis, Felix. *Muhammad Ali: The Glory Years*. New York: Miramax Books, 2003. (796.83 A398d)

Brazelton, T. Berry. *Mastering Anger and Aggression the Brazelton Way*. Cambridge, Massachusetts: De Capo Press, 2005. (155.4124 B827)

Chapter Nineteen: The Hair on the Back of Your Neck

Gladwell, Malcolm. *Blink: The Power of Thinking Without Thinking*. New York: Little, Brown and Co., 2005. (153.44 G543)

Baker, Leigh. *Protecting Your Children From Sexual Predators*. New York: St. Martin's Press, 2002. (616.8583 B167)

Chapter Twenty: The Last Day of School

Foonberg, Jay G. *Finding the Right Lawyer*. Chicago, Illinois: American Bar Association, Section of Law Practice Management, 1995. (340.029 F686)

Chapter Twenty-one: The Summer Crew

Squire, David. *The Small Garden Specialist*. London: New
Holland, 2005. (712.6 S774)

Abramovitz, Melissa. *West Nile Virus*. San Diego, California:
Lucent Books, 2004. (J 616.925 A)

Dafoe, Daniel. *A Journal of the Plague Year*. New York: Modern
Library, 2001.

Chapter Twenty-two: Love Stories

Sager, Donald J. *Small Libraries: Organization and Operation*.
Fort Atkinson, Wisconsin: Highsmith Press, 2000. (025 S129)

Potok, Andrew. *A Matter of Dignity: Changing the Lives of the
Disabled*. New York: Bantam Books, 2002. (362.4 P864)

Painter, Lucy. *Best Ever Craft Project Book*. London: Hermes
House, 2005. (745.5 B 561)

Chapter Twenty-three: Vacation Time

Penisten, John. *Kaua'i, The Garden Island*. Roseville, California:
Prima Publishing, 2001. (919.6941 P411)

Bartlett, Richard D. *Geckos: Everything About Selection, Care,
Nutrition, Diseases, Breeding, and Behavior*. Hauppauge, New
York: Barrons, 1995. (639.395 B291B)

Thomas, Craig, and Scott, Susan. *All Stings Considered: First Aid
and Medical Treatment of Hawaii's Marine Injuries*. University
of Hawaii Press, 1997. (Out of print.)

Chapter Twenty-four: Flying Saucers and Lemon Squares

Spitz, Bob. *The Beatles: The Biography*. New York: Little, Brown, 2005. (784.54 B369s)

Randles, Jenny. *The UFO Conspiracy: The First Forty Years*. New York: Barnes & Noble, 1993. (001.942 R327)

Patton, Phil. *Dreamland: Travels Inside the Secret World of Roswell and Area 51*. New York: Villard Books, 1998. (001.942 P322)

Pastor, Carol. *Pastry Magic*. New York: Wiley, 1996. (641.865 P293)

Chapter Twenty-five: Senior Librarians

Deblieux, Michael. *Supervisor's Guide to Employee Performance Reviews*. Carlsbad, California: Parker Publications, 1992. (658.3125 D286)

Machiavelli, Niccolò. *The Prince*. London: Penguin Books, 2003. (320.1.M149)

Meaney, James A. *How to Buy a Franchise*. Naperville, Illinois: Sphinx Publications, 2004. (658.8708 M483)

Chapter Twenty-six: Special Events

May, Debra Hart. *Proofreading Plain and Simple*. Franklin Lakes, New Jersey: Career Press, 1997. (686.2255 M466)

Berry, Dawn Bradley. *Domestic Violence Sourcebook*. Los Angeles: Lowell House, 2000. (362.8292 B534)

Selected Reading

LIBRARIANS LIKE BOOKS. They like to read them, critique them, order them from librarian's catalogs, and recommend them to other people and other librarians. This is normal behavior for a person in such a profession. Some books evoke a stronger response, and readers grow animated and passionate when talking about these books. When the right book is picked up at the right time, the effect can be life-changing. These are our favorite books.

Terri *(children's librarian)*

1. *Lace* Shirley Conran

2. *A Fine, Fine School* Sharon Creech

3. *The Three Investigators* (series) Alfred Hitchcock

4. *Look Book* (series) Tana Hoban

5. *Gone, But not Forgotten* Phillip Margolin

6. *Twilight* Stephanie Meyer

7. *Kiss the Girls* James Patterson

8. *The Cricket in Times Square* George Selden

9. *Romeo* Elise Title

10. *Ginnie and Geneva* (series) Catherine Woolley

Rhea *(assistant librarian and coworker at my branch for years)*

1. *The Education of Henry Adams* Henry Adams

2. *Villette* Charlotte Brontë

3. *Jerusalem Poker* Edward Whittemore

4. *The Ax* Donald Westlake

5. *Sesame and Lillies* John Ruskin

6. *The Golden Bowl* Henry James

7. *Alice in Wonderland* Lewis Carroll

Don *(assistant librarian and author)*

1. *The Man Who Mistook His Wife for a Hat* Oliver Sacks

2. *One Hundred Years of Solitude* Gabriel García Márquez

3. *Rats, Lice & History* Hans Zinsser

4. *Why Big Fierce Animals Are Rare: An Ecologist's Perspective* Paul A. Colinvaux

5. *In Patagonia* Bruce Chatwin

6. *Catch-22* Joseph Heller

7. *Spoon River Anthology* Edgar Lee Masters

8. *Giving Good Weight* John McPhee

9. *Glitz* Elmore Leonard

10. *Blood Meridian: Or the Evening Redness in the West* Cormac McCarthy

Andrea (*library page and a darn fine daughter. Getting a master's degree at UCLA in library science*)

1. *The Telling* Ursula LeGuin

2. *Bellwether* Connie Willis

3. *American Gods* Neil Gaiman

4. *An Ogre Downstairs* Diana Wynne Jones

5. *Sky Coyote* Kage Baker

6. *The Hitchhiker's Guide to the Galaxy* Douglas Adams

7. *Finder: Talisman* Carla Speed McNeil

8. *Rosencrantz and Guildenstern Are Dead* Tom Stoppard

9. *A Distant Soil* Colleen Doreen

10. *The Wasteland* T. S. Eliot

Jay (*children's librarian and coworker. Had he played his cards right, we would have written a book on the Peloponnesian War by now. Can conjugate verbs in Latin. Sensitive about Charles M. Schulz.*)

1. *Ender's Game* Orson Scott Card

2. *Charlotte's Web* E. B. White

3. *Half Magic* Edward Eager

4. *The Adventures of Huckleberry Finn* Mark Twain

5. *Whale Talk* Chris Crutcher

6. *Candide* Voltaire

7. *Devil in the White City* Erik Larson

8. *Warriner's English Grammar and Composition* John Warriner

9. *Book of Jonah* Bible (Old Testament)

10. *As You Like it, Charlie Brown* Charles M. Schulz